Pregnancy
& birth

Pregnancy
& birth

Gill Thorn

HAMLYN

For my husband, Dennis

Commissioning Editor: **Sian Facer**
Art Director: **Jacqui Small**
Executive Art Editor: **Keith Martin**
Designers: **Emma Jones and Nina Pickup**
Editors: **Mary Lambert and Jane McIntosh**
Special Photography: **Daniel Pangbourne**
Jacket Photography: **Sandra Lousada**
Stylist: **Sheila Birkenshaw**
Hair and Makeup: **Leslie Sayles**
Illustrations: **Melanie Northover**
Picture Research: **Wendy Gay**
Production Controller: **Victoria Merrington**

First published in Great Britain in 1995 by
Hamlyn, an imprint of Reed Consumer Books,
part of Reed International Books Limited,
Michelin House, 81 Fulham Road, London SW3 6RB
and Auckland, Melbourne, Singapore and Toronto

ISBN 0 600 58483 6

Produced by Mandarin Offset
Printed in Hong Kong

NOTE

While the advice and information are believed to be accurate and true at the time
of going to press neither the author nor the publisher can accept any legal responsibility or liability for any errors or omissions that may be made. The reader should
always consult a physician in all matters relating to health and particularly in
respect of any symptoms which may require diagnosis or medical attention.

Contents

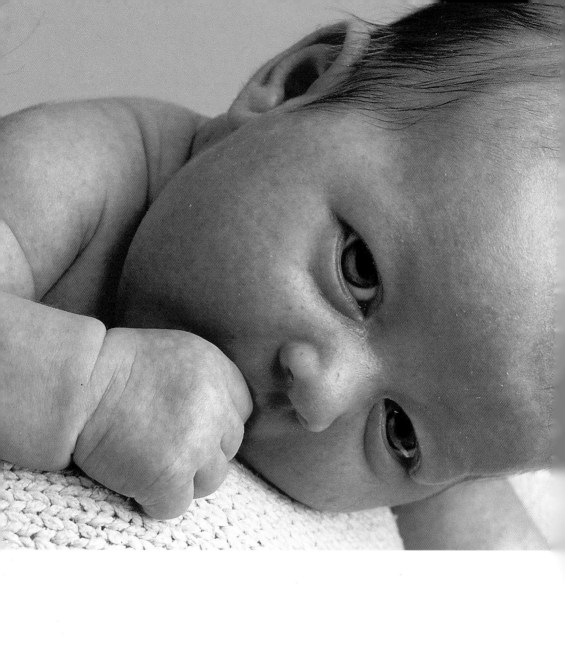

Introduction

Babies bring joy to their families but also to the wider community. It's exciting to be expecting a baby and there are many things to think about and learn. *Practical Parenting* magazine was started in 1987 to help you to enjoy this special time in your life by offering up-to-date information, reassurance and practical tips from other parents. Now there's a book to tell you all you want to know about pregnancy, birth and the early weeks with your new baby.

Most parents these days want to think about the options and share the decisions that affect them, from the type of antenatal care they receive and where their baby is born to whether labour is allowed to progress naturally or is actively managed using the latest technology. The book offers a comprehensive guide to the options available and help to make intelligent choices among them. Everyone's experience is different so it doesn't tell you what you ought to do. The decisions are up to you.

I have learned how varied the individual experience of having a baby can be from thousands of parents who have shared their joys, hopes and fears with me in more than 20 years of teaching. I'd like to acknowledge my debt to them, and to the friends who read the manuscript and made helpful comments: Sue Copello and Val Gardner, psychologist and doctor respectively and both new mothers; Helen Gill, editor of *Practical Parenting* whose sound judgement I have valued from my first contribution to the magazine soon after its launch; and my daughters Joanna and Annabel Thorn, who prevented me from taking anything for granted!

G. C. T.

1

Planning Pregnancy

‘ *Parenthood is a privilege, not a right. Thinking about why I wanted a child – the responsibilities as well as the joys – made me feel confident and ready to commit myself. I plan to enjoy pregnancy and give my baby a good start in life.* ’

WHY PLAN YOUR PREGNANCY?

It may seem calculating to plan something that is so natural such as having a baby, but thinking ahead can help you to start pregnancy in good health and a positive frame of mind. It can enhance your chances of conceiving, reduce the likelihood of problems during pregnancy, and spare you a certain amount of worry. Pregnancy today has actually never been safer but it can be an anxious time, not least because of all the information available and the tests to make sure you and the baby are alright. Thinking carefully about it in advance helps you to get everything in perspective.

Sharing the preparations for a new and exciting phase of your lives can bring you and your partner closer together. There are ups and downs and anxieties with any aspect of life and advance planning for pregnancy cannot get rid of them all, but it can make your journey smoother and help you to get the most out of a very special experience.

How you may feel about parenthood

For most women, deciding to have a baby is exciting and brings a new sense of purpose to life. You can re-enter the world of childhood in a new role, think about the little garments and nursery items to buy, and remember forgotten childhood pleasures. There is the challenge of raising a child your way, using some of your parents' tried-and-tested methods and re-inventing others. You may suddenly feel closer to friends and relatives with children, and look forward to carrying on family traditions and forming new ones.

You will probably also experience some less positive feelings. You may worry about giving up your freedom, losing out in your career, becoming dependent on your partner or just facing the responsibilities of parenthood. If you have had a miscarriage you may fear that it will happen again. You may worry about the physical demands of pregnancy, any illness that might affect your baby, or having a child with a disability. You may be concerned about being a good mother, coping with day-to-day childcare, and about how much your partner will really help you.

Any major change in life involves losses as well as gains, and a few mixed feelings will stop you viewing motherhood through rose-tinted spectacles. You will have to work through some of your doubts, but others will disappear once you are pregnant.

Your partner's feelings

Many men take great delight in young children, are proud to think of becoming a father, and are enthusiastic and eager to share the preparations. Others are pleased, but reserved about it. Like you, your partner will have moments of doubt. He may worry about being a good father, about taking on the financial responsibility for you and the baby and about your safety during pregnancy and birth. He may also be concerned about changes in your social life, your sex life and your relationship with each other.

Worries about the future can outweigh optimism when it comes to fatherhood. If your partner's reactions are lukewarm try to find out why. He may have unhappy memories of his own childhood, be afraid of the changes a baby will

'The hardest thing about having a baby was taking the plunge. We kept putting it off, first until I'd got my promotion, then until the house was straight or we'd had our holiday. There was always a good reason, but really I think we were scared of making the commitment. It seemed such a grown-up step to take. ' LIZZIE

bring, or not feel ready for the responsibilities of parenthood. Some men may feel concerned because they have no interest in babies although they like older children. Others may simply not be drawn to children at all.

All relationships are different and you may be happy to accept most of the parenting responsibility yourself. Only you can decide if you would resent this as time goes on. On the other hand, some men who are adamant that they do not want children change their minds as soon as a baby arrives!

PREPARING FOR PREGNANCY

It's never too late to improve your state of health, but if you and your partner have the chance to do so before you become pregnant, take it! Healthy parents tend to have healthy babies and fit mothers tend to experience fewer problems during pregnancy and birth.

A child will be dependent on you for many years even if you return to work, so your life will and should change; pregnancy starts the process of adaptation. It can be frustrating to find that your body slows down and you can't concentrate on much beyond your own and the baby's needs as pregnancy advances, but the less rushed, new rhythm is more suited to the needs of a baby. Many women are glad of a reason to find a slower but more satisfying pace of life. Most preparation for pregnancy is simply common sense and ideally should involve both partners. For example:

- Look at ways of reducing the stress in your life. Try to shed unnecessary work commitments or reorganize your social life.
- Go to your GP for a check-up so that you start pregnancy with a clean bill of health. Your doctor can prescribe folic acid supplements and may recommend you to take them for at least a month before becoming pregnant.
- Look at the balance between work and play, activity and relaxation, your own needs and those of others in your life. If one aspect dominates another, try to modify it.
- Concentrate on taking more exercise and improving your diet.
- Change habits you know are bad for you such as smoking and excessive drinking of alcohol.

Getting fit

The special needs of pregnancy often become obvious to women too late, when they realize how much harder everything is if they are unfit! If you increase your suppleness, strength and stamina before becoming pregnant you'll be able to carry a baby more easily, reduce the risk of backache and other discomforts, and find you get less tired. It's not wise to start a rigorous exercise programme during pregnancy and any activity that you are not used to doing should be treated cautiously. Swimming and brisk walking are safe for most women, but ask your doctor for individual advice.

Women have been discouraged from taking part in activities such as skiing and horse riding during pregnancy, but there is little evidence for a blanket ban. It depends on individual circumstances. If your pregnancy is normal and you are fit and skilled at an activity you'll probably find you can carry it on in a modified form. Marathon runner Ingrid Kristiansen competed at international level when she was seven months pregnant, but most women are content with more modest goals!

Eating healthily

Good nutrition is the basic foundation for good health. It protects the body against infection by building a strong immune system and helps rid the system of toxins. It improves the feeling of well-being and increases the chances of conceiving and having a successful pregnancy.

Research suggests that drinking more than three cups of coffee (or the equivalent) per day can delay the chance of conception. Caffeine is addictive and you may want to cut down for other reasons, such as its interference with sleep patterns and the fact that it is a diuretic.

It may seem incredible that your body can provide everything needed to grow a healthy baby using the simplest of essentials: water, oxygen and good food. Try to eat some foods like these every day to help ensure that you and your baby get the best nourishment possible.

WHOLESOME FOODS

- *Take salad items such as carrot and celery sticks to work in a plastic container, to eat with a wholemeal roll.*
- *Choose fruit or low fat yoghurt for dessert.*
- *Eat snacks of nuts, sunflower seeds, dried apricots or raisins instead of crisps and biscuits.*
- *To make the transition from white rice or flour to brown easier, mix them in equal quantities at first.*
- *Vegetables from large supermarket chains are usually very fresh. Stir-fry or steam them to retain vitamins and minerals.*
- *Buy a wholefood cookery book and try out a new recipe every week.*
- *See page 40 for foods to avoid when you're pregnant.*

A wholesome diet should include fresh vegetables and fruit, unrefined carbohydrates like wholemeal bread and brown rice, and protein such as meat, fish, milk, eggs, nuts and pulses. You should get all the vitamins, minerals and other nutrients you need from foods like these. If your diet consists mainly of processed or fat-laden foods try to improve it for your own and your future baby's sake .

Stopping contraception

If you are taking the Pill or using an intra-uterine device (IUD) you might want to use another form of contraception for about three months before attempting to get pregnant. This will allow your body to return to normal as both forms of contraception can alter the balance of nutrients such as zinc, copper and certain vitamins. Good nutrition, plus a short break from the Pill or an IUD, will help to put you in a healthy condition for pregnancy. Allowing your periods time to settle down to a regular pattern also makes dating your pregnancy much more accurate.

RISKS IN PREGNANCY

Being pregnant today may appear a risky process because bad news always gets more attention than good news. However, the risks are actually less than they used to be because women in general are better nourished, better housed, have fewer children and are able to plan when to have them more easily. These factors are very important in making pregnancy safer than it was for previous generations.

If you make yourself aware of the avoidable risks and take action to reduce them, you can get the others in proportion and relax knowing that you have done your best.

Older motherhood

Physically, the best time to have a baby is in your early 20s. However, many of the risk factors associated with giving birth when you're older could affect any woman, whatever her age; being overweight, and having had several babies or suffered infertility problems just happen to be more common in older women.

The risk of chromosomal abnormalities does increase with age (see page 55) but most problems, including heart defects, spina bifida, cleft palate and club foot, are no more common in older mothers. Some problems, for example, congenital dislocation of the hip (clicky hips), are actually less common. Keep an eye on your weight and take regular exercise to improve your fitness before becoming pregnant. There is sound evidence that older women who are fit and of average weight for their height (see chart) suffer fewer problems in pregnancy and birth. They also cope just as well physically as younger women.

If you're over 35 and smoke you are five times as likely to have a baby who suffers poor growth (see page 103) and who could have problems in early life. The risk of minor malformations in the baby is significantly increased. So it is even more important for older women to stop smoking (see page 41).

In general, the older you are the better you know yourself and the more motivated you may be to help yourself by planning ahead. You may also be more financially secure and able to get the most out of the emotional and spiritual side of pregnancy.

The right weight for your height

If you eat a balanced diet, are physically active and have plenty of energy most of the time, your weight is probably about right for you. For a more precise guide, look at the chart and convert your height into metres and your weight into kilograms. Now divide your weight by your height squared:

For example: If you weigh 10st 1lb (64kg) and are 5ft 7in (1.7m) tall:

$$\frac{\text{wt in kg}}{(\text{ht in m}) \times (\text{ht in m})} \qquad = \qquad \frac{64}{1.7 \times 1.7} \qquad = \qquad 22.15$$

A score of around 20 to 25 is the best range for pregnancy although a little more is fine. If you are generally healthy and fall within this range you will not benefit from gaining or losing weight, so concentrate on the quality of the food you eat.

Underweight women can be perfectly healthy but may find it harder to conceive. If you score under 20 you may want to eat more, or more often, to gain some weight. If you score over 30 you are at greater risk of problems such as gestational diabetes (see page 53) during pregnancy, so you might want to lose a few pounds before trying to become pregnant. Talk to your GP if you are concerned.

Weight conversion chart: st/lb to kg   1lb = 0.454kg

st	lb	kg	st	lb	kg	st	lb	kg
7	0	44.5	9	0	57.2	11	0	69.9
	1	44.9		1	57.6		1	70.3
	2	45.4		2	58.1		2	70.8
	3	45.8		3	58.5		3	71.2
	4	46.3		4	59.0		4	71.7
	5	46.7		5	59.4		5	72.1
	6	47.2		6	59.9		6	72.6
	7	47.6		7	60.3		7	73.0
	8	48.1		8	60.8		8	73.5
	9	48.5		9	61.2		9	73.9
	10	49.0		10	61.7		10	74.4
	11	49.4		11	62.1		11	74.8
	12	49.9		12	62.6		12	75.3
	13	50.4		13	63.1		13	75.8
8	0	50.8	10	0	63.5	12	0	76.2
	1	51.3		1	64.0		1	76.7
	2	51.7		2	64.4		2	77.1
	3	52.2		3	64.9		3	77.6
	4	52.6		4	65.3		4	78.1
	5	53.1		5	65.8		5	78.5
	6	53.5		6	66.2		6	79.0
	7	54.0		7	66.7		7	79.5
	8	54.4		8	67.1			
	9	54.9		9	67.6	13	0	82.6
	10	55.3		10	68.0			
	11	55.8		11	68.5	13	7	85.8
	12	56.3		12	69.0			
	13	56.7		13	69.4	14	0	89.0

Height conversion chart: ft/in to metres   1in = 2.54cm   1ft = 0.305m)

ft	in	m	ft	in	m	ft	in	m
4	8	1.42	5	2	1.57	5	8	1.72
	9	1.45		3	1.60		9	1.75
	10	1.47		4	1.62		10	1.77
	11	1.50		5	1.65		11	1.80
5	0	1.52		6	1.67	6	0	1.83
	1	1.55		7	1.70		1	1.86

'*It's a good idea to plan your pregnancy if you can. I gave up smoking before I was expecting my son, and cut out chips and burgers in favour of salads and greens.*

There are risks in everything, even in crossing the road, and you have to get them in proportion. Of course I worried when I was pregnant. It's part of caring for the baby. Basically I just follow sensible advice and use common sense. If you become paranoid you spoil that lovely special feeling you get when you're expecting a baby. ' JANICE

Smoking

Smoking is one of the main culprits in a range of pregnancy problems from miscarriage through to pre-term delivery. The major cause of infant illness and death is being born too small (see page 103). About one-third of low birthweight babies are like this because their mothers smoked during pregnancy. The risks continue as the child grows up; babies of mothers who smoked during pregnancy are less healthy, more likely to be hyperactive and more at risk from cot death.

If you continue to smoke during pregnancy you'll either choose to believe that your baby will escape harm, or you'll suffer agonizing guilt and self reproach. It's best to tackle the problem before you conceive. There are some ideas to help you stop smoking in Chapter 3.

Passive smoking also affects the developing baby, so ask your partner to give up smoking, or to smoke outside or in another room. Try to negotiate a special area for smokers in your workplace if there isn't one already.

Drugs

All illegal and addictive drugs potentially cause harm to the developing baby. We know as little about the use of marijuana and cocaine in pregnancy as was known about cigarette smoking 20 years ago, so more problems will probably be discovered. Cocaine crosses the placenta and may damage it, leading to poor fetal growth (see page 103) and some serious complications of pregnancy, including stillbirth. Long term effects for the baby include irritability, excessive crying and abnormal brain wave patterns. Marijuana can interfere with conception and has been linked with severe pregnancy sickness and complications such as abnormally long or rapid labours. It affects placental efficiency and can lead to low birthweight babies.

Medicines

Most women know not to take any pills or medicines, such as multi-vitamins, common cold remedies and pain killers including aspirin and paracetamol, without advice from a doctor or pharmacist during pregnancy. Some prescription drugs have withstood the test of time and are perfectly safe. Others, including common drugs such as tranquillizers, may carry risks to the baby. In certain cases the risk may be outweighed by the benefits of taking the drug.

If you need to take regular medication check with your doctor, who will have access to the latest information, before attempting to become pregnant.

There may be other forms of treatment or lower-risk medication that you could try. You could discuss taking smaller doses for a shorter time or using an alternative therapy, if appropriate. Women's Health (see Appendix) may provide helpful information.

MEDICAL AND PHYSICAL CONDITIONS

If you suffer from a condition such as chronic backache or have a pre-existing infection it makes sense to get it treated before you conceive. Once you are pregnant it may be harder to clear up, either because of the effects of hormones or because the appropriate medication is unsafe in pregnancy.

It's useful to find out about how pregnancy could affect any chronic medical condition you may have. Knowing what to expect can be reassuring and it's easier to look after yourself well. For example, asthmatics whose condition is well controlled usually have normal pregnancies. About two-thirds find their condition stays the same or improves, although the most severe sufferers may find that it worsens, especially after the fourth month. Diabetics who keep the disease under control have as good a chance as anyone else of having an uncomplicated pregnancy these days, provided they always follow medical advice.

Women with a physical disability often feel isolated when they are pregnant. Access to buildings, facilities and information can be restricted. Some disabled women have said that control was subtly denied and decisions taken for them, or they got the impression that they were an interesting medical condition rather than a person! You will probably have to find information for yourself (see Appendix) but planning can minimize problems and enable you to enjoy pregnancy as much as anyone else.

Genetic problems

Most people probably have a few less-than-perfect genes without knowing it. For the majority of serious genetic conditions, a baby has to inherit a faulty gene from each parent before being affected.

It's worth seeking advice if you know you're at higher risk of suffering from a particular defect. This includes regional or ethnic groups in which a condition is more prevalent, such as people of Eastern European Jewish origin for Tay-Sach's disease, and couples where one partner suffers from a congenital problem. Couples who know about an inherited disorder in either family, or who are closely related, should also seek advice.

There are about 5,000 rare single-gene defects known at present, so testing everyone randomly for them would be like looking for a needle in a haystack. Where a defect is known or suspected a genetic counsellor can give you the odds on your child being affected, help you decide whether to take the risk, and tell you if there is a test that could find out if a baby is affected.

QUESTIONS AND ANSWERS

Q: We have a smallholding and keep a few sheep, goats and chickens as well as having a sheepdog and two cats as pets. Are there any risks from looking after the animals during my pregnancy?

A: The main risk from household pets is toxoplasmosis, an infection that can damage the fetus in the early weeks of pregnancy or be passed directly to the baby in the later months, although only about one in 10,000 babies is born with it. If your pets have an active infection they could pass it to you; or you could acquire it by drinking unpasteurized milk. On the other hand you may already be immune to the disease.

Ask your doctor to test for antibodies before you become pregnant. If you are immune this will give you peace of mind; if not you could be re-tested if you develop a slight fever and swollen glands followed by a rash. Any toxoplasmosis antibodies discovered would be the result of a recent infection.

You should be careful about hygiene when caring for the farm animals. In particular, an infection that causes sheep to miscarry (*Chlamydia psittaci*) poses a similar threat to women. When you are pregnant ask someone else to milk your ewes and help with lambing. Call your GP if you experience flu-like symptoms after you have been in contact with sheep.

Q: My lifestyle is busy and my work involves a great deal of travelling. I don't always eat very well. Should I take vitamin and mineral supplements before becoming pregnant?

A: Have a word with your doctor before taking pills of any sort. As you are aware, a poor diet may not supply all the nutrients that you need, so you could start pregnancy with a deficit.

Experts have differing views about the wisdom of taking supplements, other than folic acid which is currently recommended. Some feel that food habits are hard to change but deficiencies can be avoided with a pill; others point out that excesses of certain vitamins are damaging and may rob the body of other vitamins because of the complex interactions between nutrients. There is little research into this problem as yet.

Nutrients ought to come from a healthy diet because that is how the body uses them most effectively. A poor diet plus a vitamin and mineral supplement does not equal a good diet! Even the best pill cannot supply nutrients that have not yet been isolated in food – and there may be many of these. It would be better to try to improve your eating habits before conceiving.

Q: I work in a nursery where we have a child who was damaged by rubella. Is there any way I can find out if I'm immune to this illness and if not can I be immunized before pregnancy?

A: About 85 per cent of women are immune to rubella (German measles), having already had it or been vaccinated against it. It's no longer a common disease in the community, so even if you have no immunity you are unlikely to contract it.

For peace of mind, your blood could be tested for antibodies before conception. Alternatively your GP may suggest vaccinating you just in case and advise you to delay pregnancy for three months afterwards as a precaution. Even if you were vaccinated and later discovered that you were pregnant your baby will probably be fine. Damage caused by the live virus has not been reported after vaccination.

Q: **I am 38, single, and would dearly love to have a baby. A close friend has offered to be the father provided he has no further contact with the child. As time is running out I can see the advantages to this, but what are the pitfalls?**

A: Your friend might find it hard to relinquish responsibility for his child. Although a man who donates sperm to a licensed clinic escapes the attention of the Child Support Agency, private arrangements do not. At the very least you could be under considerable pressure to name your friend. A schoolteacher in Indiana was recently ordered to pay a large sum towards his child's support even though the mother had signed a contract saying she would never claim. British courts might take a similar line.

How would you react if the baby inherited a defect, or if your friend had second thoughts and came back to make a claim on the child, for instance? Apart from this your child would one day want to know about, and possibly search for his father.

The issues are very complex and personal and you need to think them through carefully. The Family Planning Association (see Appendix) can give you information and helpful advice.

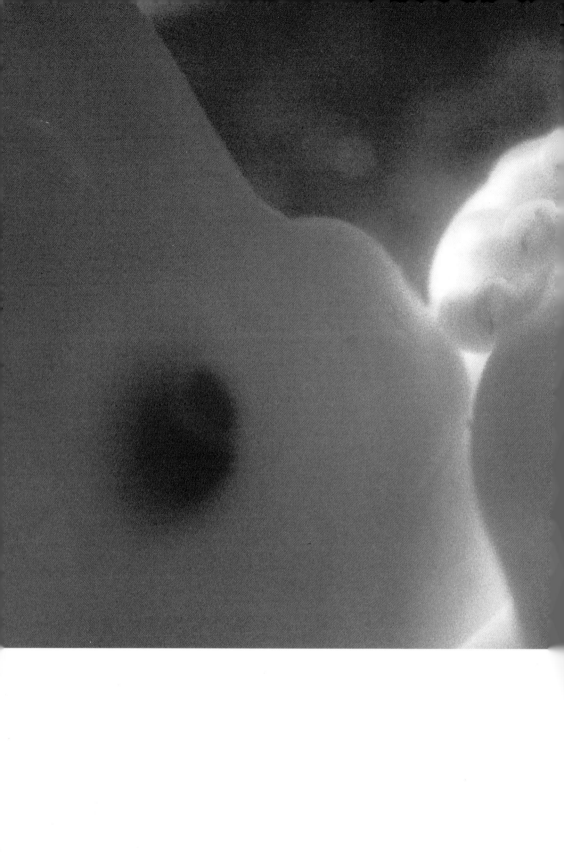

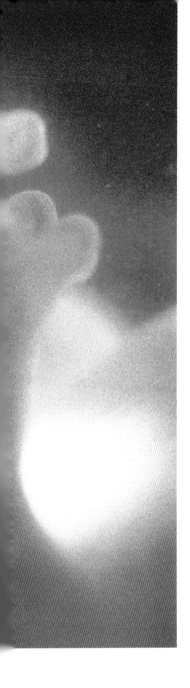

2

Conception

'I dithered on the brink of having a baby for ages, but when it happened I was bowled over! Becoming pregnant is the best thing I've ever done and I can't get the grin off my face. '

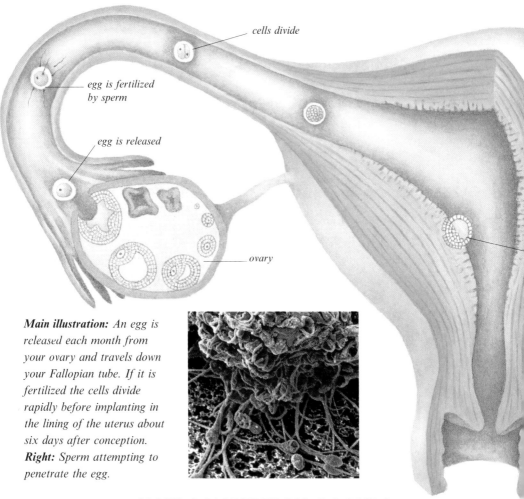

cells divide

egg is fertilized by sperm

egg is released

ovary

Main illustration: *An egg is released each month from your ovary and travels down your Fallopian tube. If it is fertilized the cells divide rapidly before implanting in the lining of the uterus about six days after conception.* **Right:** *Sperm attempting to penetrate the egg.*

HOW CONCEPTION OCCURS

About halfway through each menstrual cycle an egg is released from your ovary and drawn into the opening of your Fallopian tube. There are about 400 million sperm in each male ejaculation and they can survive for up to three days in your body. Unless the egg is fertilized within about 12 hours your body reabsorbs it. You are fertile for about four days each month.

During this period the mucus in your cervix changes to a fern-like structure through which the sperm can swim towards the egg. Many sperm take a wrong turn or get lost in the folds of the Fallopian tube, but even so thousands reach and surround the egg. When one of them penetrates its outer coating the membrane instantly changes to prevent others from following.

The victorious sperm burrows inwards until its nucleus fuses with the nucleus of the egg. Fertilization results in a single cell, smaller than this full stop. From this tiny, dynamic beginning a new life is formed.

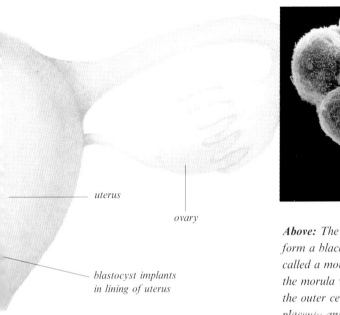

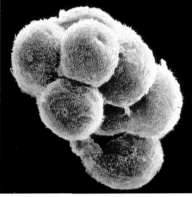

uterus

ovary

blastocyst implants
in lining of uterus

Above: *The fertilized egg divides to form a blackberry-like cluster of cells called a morula. The inner cells of the morula will form the embryo and the outer cells will become the placenta and amniotic sac.*

Twins

If two eggs are released and fertilized by separate sperm, the result is non-identical twins. If a fertilized egg splits to form two embryos, you get identical twins who will always be the same sex.

Non-identical twins (or triplets) have separate placentas and can be different sexes, like brothers and sisters who happen to share the same uterus. They are more common in families with a history of non-identical twins, women over 35 and people of African origin. The rise in multiple births, which has increased from about one per cent to almost two per cent over a generation, is largely due to the use of fertility drugs.

Identical twins share a placenta and have the same genes as they come from the same egg and sperm. About a third of twins are identical and they are equally spread throughout the population.

Genes and chromosomes

Most living cells contain deoxyribonucleic acid, better known as DNA, a substance that includes the chemical formula to make the cell individual. It resembles two strands that spiral around each other and this famous double helix is packed into each of the thousands of genes which in turn are threaded like beads into the 23 pairs of chromosomes that form the nucleus of a human cell.

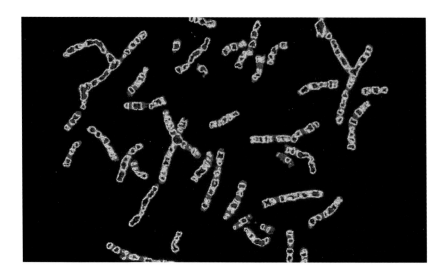

Your egg and your partner's sperm each contribute 23 chromosomes to your baby. Most chromosomes look *Chromosomes are composed mainly of the genetic material DNA.*

like a little 'x' under the microscope but the chromosome that determines sex in the sperm can be an 'x' or a 'y'. Fertilization by an 'x' sperm results in a girl while a 'y' sperm gives a boy.

DNA, genes and chromosomes are the master plan for your baby's individual characteristics, determining everything from his temperament to the colour of his eyes. Half of the thousands of bits of information come from your partner's side of the family and half from yours. Environment and life experiences will alter certain aspects of your child's physiology or personality, but his essential being is determined at the moment of conception.

CHANGES IN YOUR BODY

During pregnancy your blood supply increases, your heart works harder, your lungs expand to provide more oxygen and up to 12 pints (7 litres) of extra fluid circulates around your body.

Hormones are released to stop your periods, although your cycle can also be temporarily upset by other things such as medication, sudden weight changes, fear of pregnancy, stress, travel or exhaustion.

' It was a bit of a shock, getting pregnant so soon. I came off the Pill and never had a period. The first I knew about it was that my boobs felt firmer and blue veins showed up on them. Then I started to fall asleep as soon as I got home from work. ' MARILYN

Pregnancy hormones enable you to carry on with daily life while your baby grows and your body changes, but they also produce mood swings and some of the less welcome symptoms of early pregnancy. For example, oestrogen and progesterone relax the smooth muscles of your internal organs so that your body can adapt as your uterus grows; but they contribute to heartburn, constipation and varicose veins. Relaxin helps to make your ligaments flexible ready for the birth, but this increases the likelihood of overstraining yourself by lifting or poor posture. However, many of the discomforts caused by pregnancy hormones can be avoided (see page 72).

'Every time we saw my husband's family someone asked me when we were going to have a son. When I found out I was pregnant all I could think of at first was that I would let them down if the baby was a girl. I was so worried about it that I made myself ill.

My husband said I should take no notice of them, because it was our baby and we would welcome either a girl or a boy. He told his family that we wanted a daughter and he made me realize that you can't live to please other people all the time. I'm enjoying my pregnancy now, but I've discovered a strange craving for pickle with everything!' SHEENA

HOW YOU MAY FEEL

When you first suspect you are pregnant you may be over the moon with excitement. If you have been actively trying to conceive your success will be a cause for great celebration and will help you to make light of any minor discomforts.

However, many women feel neutral or negative about pregnancy at first. Even if it was half expected or planned, discovering that it has actually happened may be a shock. Some women take a while to realize how much they really want the baby.

If pregnancy is unwelcome you may feel guilty, anxious about telling your partner or your family, or uncertain about what to do. You may not want to think about pregnancy, and this is not a bad instinct for a week or two. Once the turmoil settles down you will be able to think more clearly. Many children in loving families were conceived at the wrong time or in the wrong circumstances. Far from being the disaster they seemed at first, unwelcome pregnancies often turn into much loved babies.

RELATIONSHIP WITH YOUR PARTNER

Some men are fascinated by the development of a baby and the progress of pregnancy. Others regard the whole process in the way that women often feel about cars: so long as it keeps going they do not wish to know what goes on under the bonnet. Although it can be disappointing if your partner feels like this, it's no more a reflection on his ability to be a good father than wielding a spanner in a car engine shows you are a good driver!

Changes usually have more impact on those who are experiencing them than the spectators. However interested your partner may be, he can only experience pregnancy through you. Even if he is less than enthusiastic about the personal details of having a baby, he will probably want to share decisions about antenatal care, tests, and the place where your baby will be born.

Along with the joy of expecting a baby there are moments when every mum-to-be wonders what she has let herself in for. Ideally your flashes of worry will coincide with your partner's moments of confidence and you'll help each other through them. But life isn't always like this! You may hit doubts together, and feel as though you are rowing a boat in opposite directions. It's scary to feel that your relationship is under strain when you need it to be strongest, but many people take time to adjust to a new future, however welcome the change.

PREGNANCY TESTS

Your doctor or family planning clinic can provide a pregnancy test, although some will make a charge for this. Many chemists also offer them for a fee, or you can buy a home test. Laboratory tests are slightly more accurate, but home tests have the advantage of speed and privacy.

Pregnancy tests differ slightly, but they work by detecting the presence of HCG (human chorionic gonadotrophin), a hormone that is secreted into your blood and passed in urine a few days after conception. If you do the test as soon as your period is overdue a positive result is more likely to be accurate. A false negative could occur because insufficient HCG is being secreted, so some kits include a second test to confirm a negative result a few days later. If your test is positive, or you still 'feel' pregnant after two negative results, visit your GP.

Announcing the news

Finding out that you are pregnant can be one of the most exciting moments of your life, comparable only to holding your baby in your arms for the first time. Like any highly charged emotional event, it makes you see the world in a different light. Although it can be tempting to shout the news of your pregnancy from the rooftops, many women wait until after the first 12 weeks or so, when there is less likelihood of miscarriage before telling the world. Others delay announcing the news until tests for fetal abnormalities (see page 55) have been completed, and some women decide not to tell their employer or workmates, at least for a while.

' I was hysterically excited when my test was positive. We went out for a meal to celebrate, and I drank orange juice virtuously all evening while my partner drank enough wine for both of us and told complete strangers he was going to be a Dad!

We'd been trying to conceive for so long that we decided not to tell anyone else except our parents, but somehow the secret got out. In no time at all everyone at work was coming up to congratulate me. ' SHARON

◆ *Remember that your body is built for pregnancy and knows exactly what to do.*

◆ *Extra rest will help you cope with the changes of early pregnancy, making it easier to handle personal relationships.*

◆ *Share your feelings about pregnancy and parenthood with your partner. Some worries disappear when brought into the open; others can be handled better by two people.*

◆ *Borrow a book or video to discover together how a baby grows from a seed as small as a grain of sand into a little person.*

◆ *Uncertainty is part of life, so get it in proportion and take pleasure together in celebrating this special time.*

◆ *Give yourself a few weeks to adjust. Women who are pregnant for the first time often feel disorientated and unsure of themselves.*

MATERNITY CARE

As soon as you know you're pregnant it's time to think about antenatal care. Your own doctor can care for you, or you can ask any GP on the obstetric list to provide maternity care. If you prefer not to use a GP, contact the Supervisor of Midwives for your area or any midwife direct. The Regional Health Information Service (see Appendix) can advise you.

You might think that labour is a long way off, but maternity care is usually linked to the type of birth you choose (see page 84). If you have your baby in hospital your entire care may take place there, and you may see different midwives in the antenatal clinic, the labour room and the postnatal wards. 'Shared care', where you attend the hospital for some checks and see your GP or community midwife for the rest, is more personal and can save tedious journeys and waiting, but you are likely to be delivered by a hospital midwife whom you have not previously met.

Most women prefer to see familiar faces, so some areas offer 'team care', where about six midwives between them undertake all your maternity care including the delivery, which could be in a hospital, a GP unit or at home. 'Domino' (domiciliary in-out) care may also be available. This means that a community (domiciliary) midwife cares for you during pregnancy, delivers your baby in hospital and continues to care for you at home shortly after-wards. If you give birth at home or in a GP unit most of your care will be provided by an individual or team midwife, at home or at a local clinic.

It's the duty of your GP (or the Supervisor of Midwives) to arrange ante-natal care that is acceptable to you. You are not obliged to accept a form of care you dislike, or treatment from someone who upsets you.

CALCULATING YOUR EXPECTED DATE OF DELIVERY

The average length of a pregnancy is 266 days, or 280 days from the start of your last menstrual period (LMP) because you conceive about 14 days later. Your expected date of delivery (EDD) is calculated as nine calendar months plus one week from this date. For example, LMP started 17 September, plus nine months = 17 June, plus seven days = baby due 24 June. To use the EDD chart, find the month and day your last menstrual period started on the top line (bold type). The month and day your baby is due is on the line below.

Your EDD is really a guide for measuring your baby's progress. It is imprecise for several reasons. Some months are longer than others; you may have a longer or shorter cycle than the 'average' of 28 days; you may bleed a little while pregnant or miss a period before conception without realizing and so on. If you don't know the date of your LMP, or if other signs such as the size of your uterus do not accord with this date, your doctor may suggest a scan (see page 56). This is the most accurate way of dating a pregnancy.

| **January** | 1 | 2 | 3 | 4 | 5 | 6 | 7 | 8 | 9 | 10 | 11 | 12 | 13 | 14 | 15 | 16 | 17 | 18 | 19 | 20 | 21 | 22 | 23 | 24 | 25 | 26 | 27 | 28 | 29 | 30 | 31 |
| *October* | 8 | 9 | 10 | 11 | 12 | 13 | 14 | 15 | 16 | 17 | 18 | 19 | 20 | 21 | 22 | 23 | 24 | 25 | 26 | 27 | 28 | 29 | 30 | 31 | 1 | 2 | 3 | 4 | 5 | 6 | 7 |

| **February** | 1 | 2 | 3 | 4 | 5 | 6 | 7 | 8 | 9 | 10 | 11 | 12 | 13 | 14 | 15 | 16 | 17 | 18 | 19 | 20 | 21 | 22 | 23 | 24 | 25 | 26 | 27 | 28 |
| *November* | 8 | 9 | 10 | 11 | 12 | 13 | 14 | 15 | 16 | 17 | 18 | 19 | 20 | 21 | 22 | 23 | 24 | 25 | 26 | 27 | 28 | 29 | 30 | 1 | 2 | 3 | 4 | 5 |

| **March** | 1 | 2 | 3 | 4 | 5 | 6 | 7 | 8 | 9 | 10 | 11 | 12 | 13 | 14 | 15 | 16 | 17 | 18 | 19 | 20 | 21 | 22 | 23 | 24 | 25 | 26 | 27 | 28 | 29 | 30 | 31 |
| *December* | 6 | 7 | 8 | 9 | 10 | 11 | 12 | 13 | 14 | 15 | 16 | 17 | 18 | 19 | 20 | 21 | 22 | 23 | 24 | 25 | 26 | 27 | 28 | 29 | 30 | 31 | 1 | 2 | 3 | 4 | 5 |

| **April** | 1 | 2 | 3 | 4 | 5 | 6 | 7 | 8 | 9 | 10 | 11 | 12 | 13 | 14 | 15 | 16 | 17 | 18 | 19 | 20 | 21 | 22 | 23 | 24 | 25 | 26 | 27 | 28 | 29 | 30 |
| *January* | 6 | 7 | 8 | 9 | 10 | 11 | 12 | 13 | 14 | 15 | 16 | 17 | 18 | 19 | 20 | 21 | 22 | 23 | 24 | 25 | 26 | 27 | 28 | 29 | 30 | 31 | 1 | 2 | 3 | 4 |

| **May** | 1 | 2 | 3 | 4 | 5 | 6 | 7 | 8 | 9 | 10 | 11 | 12 | 13 | 14 | 15 | 16 | 17 | 18 | 19 | 20 | 21 | 22 | 23 | 24 | 25 | 26 | 27 | 28 | 29 | 30 | 31 |
| *February* | 5 | 6 | 7 | 8 | 9 | 10 | 11 | 12 | 13 | 14 | 15 | 16 | 17 | 18 | 19 | 20 | 21 | 22 | 23 | 24 | 25 | 26 | 27 | 28 | 1 | 2 | 3 | 4 | 5 | 6 | 7 |

| **June** | 1 | 2 | 3 | 4 | 5 | 6 | 7 | 8 | 9 | 10 | 11 | 12 | 13 | 14 | 15 | 16 | 17 | 18 | 19 | 20 | 21 | 22 | 23 | 24 | 25 | 26 | 27 | 28 | 29 | 30 |
| *March* | 8 | 9 | 10 | 11 | 12 | 13 | 14 | 15 | 16 | 17 | 18 | 19 | 20 | 21 | 22 | 23 | 24 | 25 | 26 | 27 | 28 | 29 | 30 | 31 | 1 | 2 | 3 | 4 | 5 | 6 |

| **July** | 1 | 2 | 3 | 4 | 5 | 6 | 7 | 8 | 9 | 10 | 11 | 12 | 13 | 14 | 15 | 16 | 17 | 18 | 19 | 20 | 21 | 22 | 23 | 24 | 25 | 26 | 27 | 28 | 29 | 30 | 31 |
| *April* | 7 | 8 | 9 | 10 | 11 | 12 | 13 | 14 | 15 | 16 | 17 | 18 | 19 | 20 | 21 | 22 | 23 | 24 | 25 | 26 | 27 | 28 | 29 | 30 | 1 | 2 | 3 | 4 | 5 | 6 | 7 |

| **August** | 1 | 2 | 3 | 4 | 5 | 6 | 7 | 8 | 9 | 10 | 11 | 12 | 13 | 14 | 15 | 16 | 17 | 18 | 19 | 20 | 21 | 22 | 23 | 24 | 25 | 26 | 27 | 28 | 29 | 30 | 31 |
| *May* | 8 | 9 | 10 | 11 | 12 | 13 | 14 | 15 | 16 | 17 | 18 | 19 | 20 | 21 | 22 | 23 | 24 | 25 | 26 | 27 | 28 | 29 | 30 | 31 | 1 | 2 | 3 | 4 | 5 | 6 | 7 |

| **September** | 1 | 2 | 3 | 4 | 5 | 6 | 7 | 8 | 9 | 10 | 11 | 12 | 13 | 14 | 15 | 16 | 17 | 18 | 19 | 20 | 21 | 22 | 23 | 24 | 25 | 26 | 27 | 28 | 29 | 30 |
| *June* | 8 | 9 | 10 | 11 | 12 | 13 | 14 | 15 | 16 | 17 | 18 | 19 | 20 | 21 | 22 | 23 | 24 | 25 | 26 | 27 | 28 | 29 | 30 | 1 | 2 | 3 | 4 | 5 | 6 | 7 |

| **October** | 1 | 2 | 3 | 4 | 5 | 6 | 7 | 8 | 9 | 10 | 11 | 12 | 13 | 14 | 15 | 16 | 17 | 18 | 19 | 20 | 21 | 22 | 23 | 24 | 25 | 26 | 27 | 28 | 29 | 30 | 31 |
| *July* | 8 | 9 | 10 | 11 | 12 | 13 | 14 | 15 | 16 | 17 | 18 | 19 | 20 | 21 | 22 | 23 | 24 | 25 | 26 | 27 | 28 | 29 | 30 | 31 | 1 | 2 | 3 | 4 | 5 | 6 | 7 |

| **November** | 1 | 2 | 3 | 4 | 5 | 6 | 7 | 8 | 9 | 10 | 11 | 12 | 13 | 14 | 15 | 16 | 17 | 18 | 19 | 20 | 21 | 22 | 23 | 24 | 25 | 26 | 27 | 28 | 29 | 30 |
| *August* | 8 | 9 | 10 | 11 | 12 | 13 | 14 | 15 | 16 | 17 | 18 | 19 | 20 | 21 | 22 | 23 | 24 | 25 | 26 | 27 | 28 | 29 | 30 | 31 | 1 | 2 | 3 | 4 | 5 | 6 |

| **December** | 1 | 2 | 3 | 4 | 5 | 6 | 7 | 8 | 9 | 10 | 11 | 12 | 13 | 14 | 15 | 16 | 17 | 18 | 19 | 20 | 21 | 22 | 23 | 24 | 25 | 26 | 27 | 28 | 29 | 30 | 31 |
| *September* | 7 | 8 | 9 | 10 | 11 | 12 | 13 | 14 | 15 | 16 | 17 | 18 | 19 | 20 | 21 | 22 | 23 | 24 | 25 | 26 | 27 | 28 | 29 | 30 | 1 | 2 | 3 | 4 | 5 | 6 | 7 |

INFERTILITY

One couple in eight take over a year to conceive a baby. About half achieve a pregnancy without help and a fifth of the rest succeed after treatment. About 35 per cent of problems can be traced to the man, 35 per cent to the woman and the rest are shared by both partners.

Infertility can be caused by problems such as blocked tubes, hormone imbalances, infections and general ill health, or by factors such as fear of pregnancy or sexual difficulties. Overheating, stress or coming off the Pill can cause temporary problems. Finding that you can't conceive a baby when you want to, and when other couples seem to manage it so easily, is nothing short of anguish. However, although the problem seems to be growing so does research into potential solutions, including assistance such as in vitro fertilization (IVF). The Family Planning Association (see Appendix) has information about achieving a successful pregnancy.

ECTOPIC PREGNANCY

About one in 350 embryos implants outside the uterus, usually in a Fallopian tube. If the pregnancy were allowed to continue the tube would rupture, which could possibly lead to infertility.

The first symptom of an ectopic pregnancy is usually pain low down at one side of the abdomen, often between the sixth and twelfth week. It may be worse when you cough or move and there may be spotting or dark brown bleeding. If you have pain, tenderness or bleeding contact your GP.

If a pregnancy test is positive but an ultrasound scan (see page 56) shows no signs of pregnancy in the uterus, a laparoscopy may be performed. A fine instrument is inserted through the abdomen to look directly at the tubes. Early diagnosis and treatment can save the tube in 80 per cent of cases so that you have a good chance of conceiving again.

TO INCREASE YOUR CHANCES OF CONCEIVING:

◆ *You and your partner should make changes to your lifestyle to reduce stress caused by overwork and exhaustion.*

◆ *You and your partner should stop smoking and check your diet (see pages 12-13 and 39-41).*

◆ *Check if any chemicals you or your partner work with are linked to infertility.*

◆ *Your partner could try to avoid overheating from hot baths or tight underwear and jeans.*

◆ *If you are not pregnant after a year (six months if you are over 35) ask your GP to refer you to a specialist.*

MISCARRIAGE

Up to 40 per cent of pregnancies are thought to miscarry early on, before they are confirmed. Your reaction to a miscarriage depends on how you felt about your pregnancy, but it causes grief and considerable loss of confidence to many women. However, the chances are strongly in your favour when a pregnancy has been confirmed as at least 85 per cent of these continue successfully.

An abnormal embryo is the most likely cause of miscarriage in the first 10 weeks. Investigations to find a cause are usually only considered after three successive early miscarriages. This seems hard, but it's an expression of confidence that there is unlikely to be a problem and you have just been unlucky.

Miscarriages between 12 and 20 weeks occur in one to two per cent of pregnancies, but are rare where everything is otherwise normal. A fifth to a quarter of late miscarriages may be caused by the cervix opening too soon, possibly due to damage from surgical treatment or a previous birth. If you have suffered such a tragedy in the past your cervix may be closed with a stitch at 12-16 weeks to help support it.

Most women experience aches, cramps or light spotting at some stage during pregnancy without there being a problem. Emotional upsets, minor falls, sex and things like lifting toddlers or shopping do not usually cause miscarriages, but if you have a history of them your GP may suggest avoiding such activities.

Vaginal bleeding could indicate a threatened miscarriage. Some doctors advise extra rest but there is no evidence that it makes any difference. If nothing else happens the chances of your pregnancy continuing are high, with no extra risk of abnormality in the baby.

If you have a history of miscarriage, if bleeding or pain are severe, or if you pass clots or other material, seek immediate treatment from a doctor or the nearest hospital. Otherwise, contact your GP if you are worried or have any of these symptoms:

- Cramps accompanied by bleeding.
- Pain that is severe or lasts over 24 hours without bleeding.
- Bleeding that is as heavy as a normal period.
- Light spotting or staining continuing for more than three days.

After a miscarriage

Miscarriage happens to lots of women and most go on to have a baby successfully. After an early miscarriage you may be offered a D & C: the neck of the uterus is gently dilated and the lining scraped or aspirated to make sure nothing remains to cause infection. Some doctors suggest waiting three to six months before trying to conceive again (although lovemaking can resume before this) to give yourself time to recover physically and emotionally. The Miscarriage Association (see Appendix) can offer advice and support.

QUESTIONS AND ANSWERS

Q: I was shocked to discover that I was pregnant as I didn't feel ready for a baby. My partner blamed me for missing my pill and we had some spectacular rows before coming to our senses. Now we are looking forward to becoming parents, but I'm overwhelmed with guilt and fear. Could our baby have been affected by the stress we were under at first?

A: Unexpected pregnancies are not always welcome and it can be hard to relate to a baby and imagine yourselves as parents at first. Couples often think and say things that they later regret. Emotional stresses do affect the fetus but unless they are severe and prolonged they are unlikely to make more than a temporary impression. A baby only learns when he reaches the right stage of maturity for a particular experience. In the early months he is both emotionally and physically immature.

Although many studies have been carried out, there is no sound, direct evidence to suggest that emotional stress affects a baby adversely before birth. Indirect evidence suggests that the fetus is exposed to the sort of stress levels that he will have to learn to handle in everyday life, but is protected from excess stress. Most women will have some negative thoughts or a few rows during pregnancy. The positive feelings you now have about your pregnancy are probably more significant.

Q: We would like to have a daughter. Is there any way to boost our chances, and could we find out our baby's sex before birth?

A: Investigations such as ultrasound scans and amniocentesis (see page 57) can usually determine whether you are carrying a boy or a girl, but they are not always correct and would not be used for choosing the sex of your baby.

There is a new technique where 'x' (male) and 'y' (female) sperm are separated in the laboratory and artificial insemination is carried out to increase the chances of conceiving the desired sex. The Family Planning Association (see Appendix) can give you more information.

Other suggestions for increasing your chances of having a girl or a boy are less expensive but require more dedication. In 1979 doctors in a Paris maternity hospital claimed an 80 per cent success rate with a special diet. To conceive a girl the mother ate food that included starch and milk products, raw or frozen vegetables, unsalted butter, and fruit with the exception of pineapple, peaches and prunes. For a boy the diet had to be rich in salty foods, meat and fruit, and include dried vegetables and salted butter.

Another theory holds that timing intercourse is important because female sperm swim slowly but live longer than male sperm. Couples who want a girl should have intercourse two days before ovulation, so that most of the 'x' sperm will have died before the egg arrives. For a boy you should have intercourse on the day an egg is released, so that faster-swimming male sperm are more likely to fertilize it. Of course it is not always easy to know when an egg will be released. You can buy a special thermometer at the chemist to pinpoint ovulation, but would need to keep a record of your temperature for several months beforehand for it to have any degree of accuracy.

It can be fun to try to influence the sex of your baby, but don't pin your hopes on methods that can never be foolproof! Most parents are happy to welcome a boy or a girl into their family.

Q: My doctor says that I have a retroverted uterus. Will this make it harder to conceive, and does it affect pregnancy?

A: The uterus is usually tipped forward towards your pubic bone with its upper segment above your bladder. The position of a retroverted uterus is more upright, lined up with your spine. About 17-20 per cent lie naturally in this position. Very occasionally the uterus becomes retroverted as a result of disease or pelvic infection; these could cause infertility rather than the position of the uterus.

For most women with a retroverted uterus, conception is no less likely and miscarriage no more likely than for anyone else. The uterus usually moves forward spontaneously somewhere between the ninth and twelfth week and the pregnancy is just like any other.

Q: Our baby was conceived shortly before our holiday in Greece. Not knowing, I happily ate the local seafood and drank rather a lot of wine. I've had no problems but I feel guilty now as my baby's organs were forming. Is it likely that they have been harmed?

A: It's possible, but unlikely. Many actions increase a risk without turning it into a certainty. Drinking too much and eating seafood are *potential*, not inevitable causes of harm. An embryo that is damaged during the early stages of development is often miscarried, so your healthy pregnancy suggests that your baby is probably unaffected by anything you did on holiday.

It's hard to avoid all theoretical hazards, even after you have become pregnant. Your protective feelings about your baby are designed to be a positive influence on what you do from now on, not to make you feel guilty about risks you took before you knew you were pregnant.

Q: A friend says it is dangerous to have a high temperature in early pregnancy as the baby can be affected. How can I avoid it and what should I do if I get a fever?

A: An increase in body temperature to over 104°F (40°C) for a day, or over 102°F (38.5°C) for two days or more, *may* cause birth defects particularly between the third and seventh weeks of pregnancy.

You cannot isolate yourself from everyday life in case you catch something! Thousands of women who had flu or some other illness before realizing they were pregnant have gone on to have healthy babies. A strong immune system built on a good diet and a sensible lifestyle will help to protect you from infections.

If you have a high temperature, say over 101°F (38°C), don't take any home remedies. Contact your GP, who may suggest bringing it down by sponging yourself with tepid water or having a cool bath, although you should stop if you shiver. Other treatment would depend on how high your temperature was and your doctor's advice.

Q: I've read that VDUs can cause miscarriages and birth defects, and I work in an open plan office full of them. Is it true, and if so can anything be done about it?

A: No pregnancy related problems have been reported among women who use VDUs for 20 hours a week or less. Even if you work full time some experts say that modern equipment emits such low levels of radiation that they could not possibly harm a fetus, and that stress in the working situation may be more significant. But talk to your company's medical officer if there is one. Some employers have agreements that allow women who have worked with the firm for a certain length of time to move to other work during pregnancy.

More radiation is emitted from the back of a VDU than the screen, so if your desk is near someone else's VDU you could ask to be moved. Don't strain to see the screen and have a break away from your desk for a few minutes every hour. Perhaps you could alternate VDU work with other work during the day.

3

Early
Pregnancy

(Months 1–3)

‘ *When I was first pregnant I felt
such pride, as though I'd grown up and
proved myself at last. But then came
the fears. Did I want to give up my
freedom, would I be a good mother,
could I bear the sleepless nights, or the
pain of the birth? The first three
months crept by, with sickness and
self-doubt, and indescribable joy at the
new life I was secretly nurturing.* ’

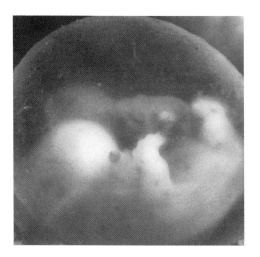

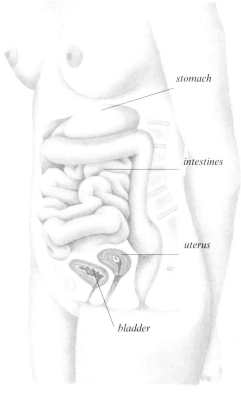

Above: An embryo at seven weeks, protected in the fluid-filled amniotic sac. All the organs of a future adult are beginning to function.
Right: First month: Your internal organs are in the same position as before conception.
Second month: Hormones soften your ligaments so that your organs can adapt as your uterus grows.
Third month: Your pregnancy may barely show but already your uterus has doubled in size.

ONE MONTH

HOW YOUR BABY DEVELOPS

After conception, the cells of your fertilized egg divide rapidly and roll down the Fallopian tube, increasing in size like a snowball. Seven days later (week three of pregnancy), dozens of cells of different shapes and sizes form a cluster. The outer layer of cells becomes the placenta and amniotic sac and the inner layer becomes the baby.

The cluster of cells (blastocyst) attaches to the lining of the uterus (endometrium) with tiny projections (villi), like ivy clinging to a wall. As the cells multiply an embryo forms, about the size of this full stop. By the fifth week the embryo is a three-layered disc as big as a lentil. The inner layer will become the baby's lungs, intestines, bladder and digestive system. The middle layer will form her heart, genitals, kidneys, bones and muscles; and the outer layer will form her brain, nervous system, external features and skin.

The embryo's head and brain develop first, followed by her body and then her limbs. By six weeks she's roughly the size of a grain of rice and her heart

36

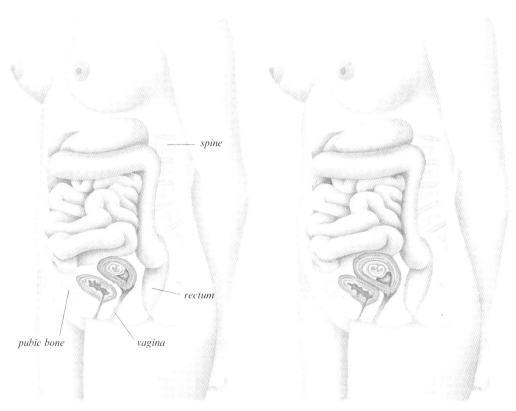

spine

rectum

pubic bone   vagina

TWO MONTHS   THREE MONTHS

has started to beat. By eight weeks she's the size of a peanut. Tiny limbs and muscles develop. A week later eyes and ears have formed and her fingers and toes are almost separated. When you are 10 weeks pregnant your embryo is about as long as the top joint of your little finger, and all her main body parts including the bones are formed. Finishing touches such as eyelids and finger nails are added. Twelve weeks after conception (week 14 of pregnancy) everything is beginning to function. Even egg (or sperm) cells are present.

HOW YOU MAY FEEL

If you are thrilled to be pregnant and your hormones cause little discomfort you may feel fitter and happier than ever before, and have glowing skin and shining hair. But many women experience mixed feelings in the early weeks. Although there is little to show and the outside world may be unaware of your pregnancy, enormous physical and emotional changes are taking place.

Periods of change can be stressful and unsettling. It takes time to adjust to having a baby, especially if it is unexpected or unwelcome. The demands that pregnancy makes on your body can sap your energy and make you feel exhausted. Hormone activity may cause symptoms that are distressing for you but are not considered important by anyone else because they don't harm the baby. Your feelings may swing from joy and excitement to self-doubt or despair. Common symptoms of early pregnancy include:

- A bloated, irrational feeling like pre-menstrual tension.
- Tender breasts, or painful nipples in cold weather.
- Flushes of heat or dizziness in stuffy rooms.
- A taste for strong flavours such as orange juice or pickles.
- Nausea, vomiting, or distaste for certain smells or foods.
- A need to urinate more frequently, caused by your growing uterus pressing on your bladder.
- Digestive upsets such as constipation or flatulence.
- Excessive saliva or a metallic taste in the mouth.
- Breakthrough bleeding when your period would have been due.
- Lifeless hair and greasy skin, or spots.
- Pulling pains at the sides of the abdomen, caused by the round ligaments stretching as the uterus moves into the abdomen.

RELATIONSHIP WITH YOUR PARTNER

Once a baby is on the way the relationship between you and your partner is bound to alter as you adjust to new roles. Many couples worry about this, but change is not necessarily negative.

Pregnancy may bring you and your partner closer together as you share new and exciting hopes for the future. Many fathers-to-be are both practically and emotionally supportive. However, if your partner seems bewildered or unhelpful try to talk to him about it. He may not understand your needs or why you feel the way you do. He may find it hard to adjust to your pregnancy. You become the focus of everyone's attention and he is expected to support you, but he may have his own worries. Some men feel proud of the pregnancy but ambivalent about becoming a father. Life will change and your partner may be anxious about the commitment required, new responsibilities and the loss of freedom. About 10 per cent of men suffer from symptoms of mild anxiety such as toothache, that are severe enough to make them seek help.

Accepting and talking about each other's feelings really does help. Try setting aside half an hour a week, with five minutes each to express your feelings without interruption and 20 minutes to discuss anything else that comes up. You'll learn more about each other, and you'll build a framework that makes it easier to deal with sensitive issues before they become damaging resentments that may threaten your relationship.

Relationship with your family

Babies bring great joy to the wider family. They provide a chance for other women to recall the special time when their own children were tiny, and men to take an interest they may have missed out on a generation ago. If you and your partner have children from previous liaisons your new baby will be a brother or sister to all of them, which can build positive bridges and help bring families together.

It will give other family members great pleasure if you share your pregnancy as far as possible. Phone them with news if they live far away; send them photocopies if you have a scan picture; find patterns you like if an auntie wants to knit bootees! If you are overwhelmed with offers to buy equipment explain that you prefer to wait until you have decided what you need. Meanwhile, it costs nothing to smile and say 'thank you'.

You may find yourself sensitive to unwanted advice and comments, but try to take them all in your stride. It's good to listen to other people's views, but deciding what is right for your baby is your responsibility, however well-meaning and experienced other family members may be. Family ties change, especially when you are expecting your first child, but with give and take new and rewarding relationships can be built.

YOUR LIFESTYLE

A healthy lifestyle means you're more likely to have a trouble-free pregnancy and a healthy baby. It's worth taking a look at your daily routine. Small changes can have a really positive effect for both you and the baby.

What to eat

If your diet is good you are more likely to have healthy blood, supple skin and muscles that function efficiently. The old saying, 'you are what you eat' applies equally to you and your baby. The early months of pregnancy when the baby's organs are developing are especially important. Mothers who eat a good or excellent diet are much less likely to have sickly, premature or low birthweight babies.

It's not really possible to give detailed instructions about what you should eat because nutritional needs differ with age, build, metabolic rate and so on. As a rough guide, you might aim to eat three to five portions of protein foods, plus five portions of bread and cereals and five of fruit and vegetables daily. Leafy green vegetable are especially valuable as they contain folic acid which is important for cell reproduction.

You gain more nutrients from fresh, whole foods than from processed foods. Try to eat some raw food, something containing iron, such as meat, nuts or dried fruit, and about four servings of calcium rich foods such as milk or milk products every day. Your body needs some fat, but fat is hidden in many foods

FOOD PRECAUTIONS

◆ *Avoid soft and blue-veined cheeses, unpasteurized milk or cheese, shellfish, cook-chill foods, uncooked egg (in meringue or mayonnaise, for example), paté and undercooked meat, to reduce the risk of infection caused by listeria or salmonella bacteria. Liver should also be avoided during pregnancy because it contains high concentrations of vitamin A which could harm the baby.*

◆ *Buy ready-prepared food from a reputable source.*

◆ *Cook home-prepared foods thoroughly (especially re-heated foods).*

◆ *Check that the temperature of your fridge is below 39°F (4°C).*

◆ *Store raw meat separately from other foods.*

◆ *Wash all fruit and vegetables before eating.*

---

and is high in calories, so two servings of butter, margarine or oil per day is adequate. If you eat poorly one day, try to make up for it the next day.

The chances are that you already think your diet is reasonably good, but look at the labels when you're shopping. Some foods are more efficient sources of nutrients than others. For example, a pint of semi-skimmed or skimmed milk gives you the same amount of protein but fewer calories and more calcium than whole milk.

Alcohol

Considerable research shows that drinking too much alcohol is harmful to your child. The baby is unlikely to be affected if you have an occasional glass of sherry, or a glass or two of wine each week, but cut down if you drink heavily and never binge. Your baby is at greater risk from one heavy drinking session than if you have a small gin and tonic every evening. No one can say what is 'safe' for an individual, so many women prefer not to drink at all when pregnant. Others drink spritzers (half mineral water) or allow themselves the occasional drink as a treat. Contact Alcohol Concern (see Appendix) for advice if you're at all worried about your current drinking habits.

'Nobody can see that you're pregnant in the early weeks. I was so proud I wanted to shout it from the rooftops, and when I found out it was twins I grinned from ear to ear all the way home! I felt so special and people were excited in a way they usually aren't when it's not your first baby. Of course there were moments of panic and my husband was a bit worried as to how we'd cope. But I was so determined to enjoy this pregnancy. ' PAULINE

Smoking

Smoking is a habit as well as an addiction. Don't despair if you find it hard to give up, but keep on trying. Ask your GP to refer you to a 'Stop Smoking' group, or contact QUIT (see Appendix) for help.

AVOIDING RISKS

One of the down sides to any pregnancy is worry. The world can seem a dangerous place when you become aware of the growing list of what pregnant women should avoid! However, most babies are born healthy even when their mothers have been exposed to risks. Worrying about things you have no control over, or that happened in the past is pointless.

Just be sensible and avoid unnecessary risks:

- Avoid chemicals such as rain-proofing sprays for anoraks and tents, paint fumes, hair dyes, pesticides and other garden sprays. Traditional cleaning fluids are probably harmless but avoid substances with any toxic warnings on the can. If you live in a farming area ask to be notified before crops are sprayed.
- Cats or dogs may carry active toxoplasmosis (see page 18). Pet lovers often develop immunity to this disease, but use rubber gloves to empty litter trays, or ask someone else to do it. Wear gloves for gardening and wash all home-grown fruit and vegetables as carefully as you would shop-bought produce.
- Avoid excess heat from very hot baths, saunas, electric blankets, heating pads or over-enthusiastic workouts.
- Have appliances such as your fridge (for safety of food storage), and microwave checked over to make sure they are all working properly. With your microwave always follow the manufacturer's instructions accurately and avoid standing in front when it's working.
- Tell the dentist or X-ray technician if you are or could be pregnant, although experts say modern low-dose diagnostic X-ray equipment rarely causes harm to the fetus.

REDUCE THE SMOKING RISK

◆ *Link your decision to stop smoking with an emotional incident. Many women use the joyful discovery that they're pregnant.*

◆ *Change your normal routine. Go for a brisk walk in the fresh air, or set yourself a task to complete when you would normally smoke a cigarette. Have a mint instead of a cigarette after a meal.*

◆ *Cut down by smoking half a cigarette and deliberately stubbing it out.*

◆ *Avoid smoke-filled rooms and smoking areas in public transport and restaurants. Ask your partner to go outside if he wants to smoke.*

◆ *Pay attention to what you eat, because an excellent diet gives some protection against the ill effects of passive smoking.*

◆ *Contact your Trades Union or Health and Safety representative at work if other people's smoking is a problem.*

HOW TO RELAX

◆ *Watch your posture (see page 44) to prevent causing unnecessary tension in your muscles.*

◆ *To relax your shoulders, pull them down and let go. They'll settle into a relaxed position. Check them every time you wait for the kettle to boil.*

◆ *Loosen your fingers. Tension from clenched hands travels up your arms and into your shoulders.*

◆ *Your face will reflect tension in your body. Relax the muscles around your eyes. Part your lips slightly and gently close them to relax your jaw and mouth.*

◆ *Buy a relaxation tape and spend some time each day learning the art of relaxing at will.*

Learn to relax

At this point, being pregnant may seem so full of pitfalls that it seems impossible to relax even for a minute! But life is full of risks and most people manage to come through unscathed. Certain environmental risks are unproven while others account for only a tiny proportion of birth defects or pregnancy complications. It's far more important to eat a good diet, have regular antenatal checks and avoid smoking or taking non-prescribed drugs. Try to get risks in proportion instead of feeling anxious and guilty over every little transgression. Do your best and then you can relax mentally.

Many women feel exhausted around the second and third months of pregnancy. Even after a good night's sleep they doze at their desk at work or fall asleep over the evening meal. It may not be easy to relax physically when you're working or looking after a lively toddler, but try to pace yourself during the day. Make allowances for the unseen changes of pregnancy and don't push yourself, especially if you're feeling under the weather. It's better to decline an invitation or make a meal from the freezer than end up feeling utterly frazzled. Many women feel guilty if they sit down without having a good excuse, but growing a baby is the best possible reason to rest.

'*When I became pregnant my life changed overnight. I didn't resent the changes, but I felt ill, emotional and mixed up and had no idea how to help myself or where to go for advice. I assumed if you had morning sickness you'd wake up, be sick and it would be over, whereas mine lasted all day. I lost weight and felt totally different inside. My partner was very supportive but he didn't understand why I cried all the time.*

I couldn't relate to a baby as it all seemed too remote. Everyone was delighted, but I had little enthusiasm because I felt so awful. I thought there must be something wrong with me. I didn't realize that other women also felt emotionally drained or found life very difficult in the early weeks. ' FRANCESCA

COPING WITH PREGNANCY SICKNESS

It's little comfort, but the first known record of this complaint is in a papyrus dated 2,000 BC, and some form of it is suffered by up to 70 per cent of women! It may be caused by the hormone HCG (human chorionic gonadotrophin) which is produced a few days after conception, reaches a peak at about 10 weeks and usually drops dramatically after 12-16 weeks.

Pregnancy sickness ranges from mild nausea in the mornings for a few weeks to severe nausea and vomiting lasting all day, in some cases throughout the entire pregnancy. It is often trivialized because it does not affect the baby adversely, but if you suffer badly from it you deserve everyone's sympathy and understanding.

Stress makes symptoms worse, but psychological factors such as 'unconscious rejection of the baby' are no longer thought to play a major role in the problem; neither is diet although there may be links with certain minerals and vitamins, especially B6.

Sickness is often worst at the time when your baby's organs are forming, so never take over-the-counter remedies without professional advice. This includes herbal or homeopathic preparations and vitamin supplements. If you cannot keep anything down you should certainly tell your doctor.

Otherwise, some of these suggestions may help:

- Accept the nausea and change your lifestyle temporarily. Ask your partner to do the cooking. Slow down, take extra rest, get fresh air every day and go to bed early.
- Don't worry about your diet for the time being. Eat little and often, whatever you can keep down. Take snacks like ginger biscuits or tiny sandwiches to eat at work.
- Sucking boiled sweets or crystallized ginger may banish the metallic taste in your mouth. Try root ginger in cooking.
- Ice lollies, plain water, fizzy drinks or herb teas may help.
- Find somebody to listen to your worries and to give practical help when you feel awful. There may be no remedy for your misery except time, but you need support to live through it.

ACHES AND PAINS

In early pregnancy the action of hormones softens all your ligaments so that as your baby grows your uterus can move out of your pelvic basin into your abdominal cavity. Ligaments that would normally stabilize your joints are softened too, and can be strained by poor posture when standing, sitting or lifting. Tense shoulder muscles, weak abdominal or buttock muscles, and wearing high heels that tilt your pelvis can cause backache. To avoid strains, watch your posture carefully, sleep on a supportive mattress, and roll onto your side before getting up.

Looking after your back

Pregnancy is an excellent time to review how you use your body. If you have picked up bad postural habits over the years it will take thought at first. However, good posture quickly becomes automatic, avoiding aches and pains.

Standing: Keep your back upright with your shoulders relaxed, pelvis balanced and feet apart. Don't rest with your weight on one hip or stick your bump out.

Lifting: Bend your knees and keep your back straight. Try not to lift and twist at the same time – move your feet instead. Keep the weight close to your body unless it's as light as this empty bucket.

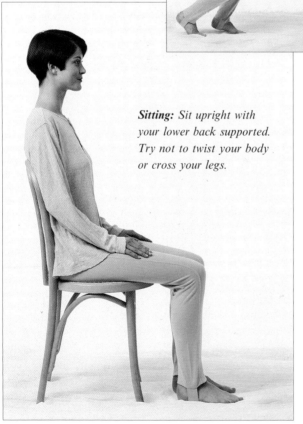

Sitting: Sit upright with your lower back supported. Try not to twist your body or cross your legs.

YOUR PELVIC FLOOR

If there is one part of the body that all women should know about it's the pelvic floor, the muscles between your legs that form the base of the pelvic basin. To locate them, look at the illustration below. Cough into your hand and you'll feel the muscles bulge a little.

They are important because they support your bladder, vagina and bowel, and control their sphincters or exits. They carry the growing weight of your uterus and baby and withstand the extra pressure when your baby's head engages (see page 52) before labour. When your baby is born the muscles guide her head to align it with your pubic arch and stretch to let her emerge. They need to be strong but flexible.

During pregnancy your pelvic floor sags a little with the extra weight, but muscles with good tone (the normal firmness of healthy tissue) return to their normal horizontal state after the birth. Over a long period, lax muscles allow your pelvic organs to change position, making it harder for the supporting muscles to function properly. This could lead to problems such as stress incontinence.

How to tone your pelvic floor

Breathing normally, slowly draw up the muscles, hold them momentarily, and release them gently. Repeat this six times, several times every day without using your abdominal and buttock muscles. Concentrate on becoming more aware of the sensations you feel. Some women find it easiest to lean forward with their knees apart and their buttocks resting on the edge of a chair seat.

Imagine that your pelvic floor is a lift in a department store. Tighten it up, pausing at each floor before moving to the next one. You may reach the second floor or the seventh depending on how much control you have. Try to stop at each floor on the way down again!

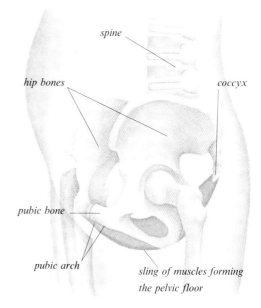

spine

hip bones

coccyx

pubic bone

pubic arch

sling of muscles forming the pelvic floor

Your pelvic floor muscles are more complex, but this shows its hammock-like structure which supports your internal organs. From front to back it has three openings – the urethra leading from the bladder, the vagina from the uterus and the anus from the bowel.

45

RIGHTS AND BENEFITS

If you work during pregnancy you have legal rights that protect your health and job, and entitlements to cash benefits when you stop work to have your baby. Some apply to all pregnant women in paid employment; for example the right to paid time off for antenatal care. This includes antenatal classes although you may need a letter from your GP or midwife stating that classes are part of your care.

Others, such as rights to move from a job involving heavy lifting to a suitable alternative if one is available, and to return to your job after your baby is born, depend on qualifying employment periods. Maternity Allowance and sickness benefits depend on contributions in a qualifying period, so you may still be eligible if you are self-employed or have recently stopped work.

All pregnant women are entitled to free prescriptions and dental care. If you are on a low income you may be able to claim free milk and vitamins, help with fares to hospital and a lump sum to buy things for the baby.

There are set times to claim in order to preserve some rights but the rules are complicated. Ask your GP, midwife or local Benefits Agency (address in phone book) for leaflets FB8 Babies and Benefits and NI 17A A Guide to Maternity Benefits. Note all the important dates in your diary.

Some employers offer better maternity benefits than required by law, so find out the terms that apply to you. The Maternity Alliance (see Appendix) has free leaflets on your rights at work, including one on redundancy.

YOUR PREGNANCY PLANNER – MONTHS 1-3

◆ *Antenatal check-ups: appointments are usually once a month after the first eight weeks of pregnancy although they may be less frequent if everything is normal. Ask about special tests for fetal abnormality (see page 55).*

◆ *Stop smoking, cut down on alcohol and make improvements to your diet now – it's important for you and your baby. If you need help there are useful addresses in the Appendix.*

◆ *If you are uncertain about your rights at work contact the Maternity Alliance (see Appendix) for information.*

◆ *Take advantage of free dental care to visit your dentist for a check up.*

◆ *Tell your employer when you need time off for antenatal care.*

◆ *Start thinking about various birth options and getting information about different hospitals (see page 85) and antenatal classes (see page 79).* Practical Parenting *magazine has up-to-date articles to help you to make choices.*

◆ *Look in the small advertisements for addresses to order maternity wear catalogues.*

QUESTIONS AND ANSWERS

Q: My back has always been one of my weak spots and I don't want to suffer during pregnancy. Apart from watching my posture is there anything I can do to help myself avoid backache problems?

A: You could strengthen your back muscles with gentle pelvic rocking. Stand with your feet apart and your knees bent. Tighten your buttocks and tilt your pelvis forwards, then release them and tilt it backwards, rocking it slowly and rhythmically. This movement also helps existing backache.

If you get backache under your shoulder blades, circle your shoulders to release stiffness. Try wearing a larger size of bra or let the hooks out, and make sure that you sit with your back straight and supported. For pain that is low down and to one side of your spine (probably a strained sacroiliac ligament) ask your partner to massage the area firmly and apply some gentle heat.

Q: I have been a vegetarian for 10 years but am now a vegan. Is this diet adequate for pregnancy, or should I take supplements?

A: Vegetarians who are healthy and eat a good, varied diet do not usually need supplements, as their blood mineral levels fall within normal ranges. Some nutritionists recommend that vegans take supplements of vitamin B12, vitamin D, calcium and iron during pregnancy, but check with your doctor first. You may also need to make sure that you get enough protein.

Vegetarians and vegans have the same needs as other pregnant women and any diet is only as good as you make it. Contact the addresses in the Appendix if you need more information.

Q: I'm delighted to be pregnant but I'm having nightmares about the birth. We were shown a film at school and although it was years ago the memory is still vivid. How can I overcome my fear?

A: The feelings and emotions that are part of giving birth, and can make it a special experience, rarely come over in films. In real life giving birth is not in vivid Technicolor and it's *your* baby, which makes a world of difference.

When negative thoughts float into your mind try not to dwell on them, but replace them with positive ones. For example, remind yourself that women are designed to give birth; that you won't be entering a competition or giving a performance, just doing your best. Concentrate on enjoying your pregnancy and looking forward to seeing your baby. The birth is simply the bridge between the two.

It's not too soon to look for antenatal classes (see page 79) to attend later on, as good ones often get booked up early. Part of the job of a parentcraft teacher is to explain about birth more fully and teach you ways of coping. After you have been to classes and as the birth gets closer you'll probably wonder why you ever felt so afraid.

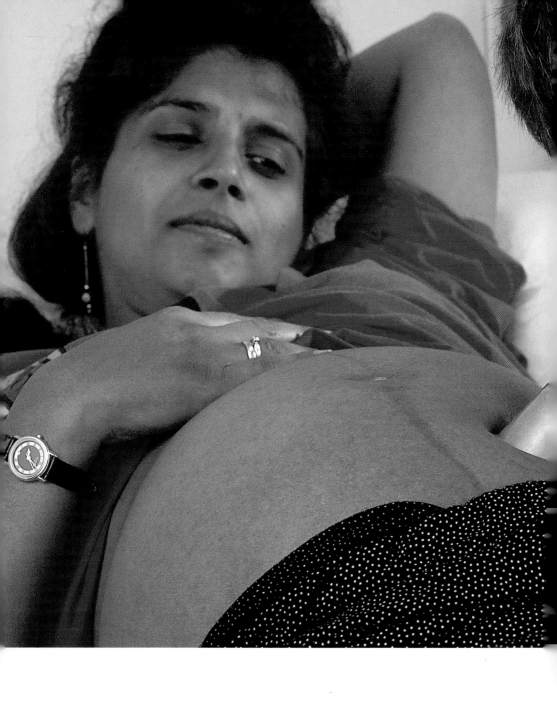

4

Antenatal Care

' Getting to know my way around the system was like learning the ropes in my first term at secondary school. I scarcely knew what I was doing but I was bowled along in a friendly way while I asked questions and learned new names for familiar things. '

WHAT IS A 'NORMAL' PREGNANCY?

Your pregnancy is normal if it progresses like the majority of pregnancies, and if any unusual symptoms you get are not generally thought to be harmful to mothers or babies. What is considered normal depends to some extent on the experience of the people concerned and on current scientific interests.

Routine antenatal checks distinguish harmless symptoms from potentially dangerous ones, so that you and your baby stay healthy and any problems are picked up early. They also give you a chance to ask questions and find out enough information to help you make informed decisions.

Pregnancy is a state of health with just an occasional problem, although doctors sometimes forget this! If you are never singled out for special attention you can rest assured that everything is going well. Even if closer attention is paid to a particular symptom it does not always mean there is a problem. Women are so individual that something could be abnormal for some women, but be normal for you.

ANTENATAL VISITS

Antenatal checks are usually carried out by a midwife, each month until the 28th week of pregnancy, then each fortnight until the 36th week and then weekly until your baby is born. You may have more checks if your pregnancy is unusual. Women with normal pregnancies often have fewer checkups but contact your doctor or midwife between visits if you have any worries.

Your partner can attend your check-ups; the first (or booking visit) is usually longer than later ones. The midwife takes your history, recording details such as your job, your lifestyle, your past and present health plus that of your partner and both families if possible. The aim is to find out your individual circumstances and anything that could affect your pregnancy. Previous pregnancies, terminations or adoptions will be noted, but say if you don't want something written down.

Your height and weight may be checked, although some doctors question whether this is useful. The weigh-in gives a baseline for later visits. Failure to put on weight could mean your baby isn't growing properly and a sudden weight gain could indicate fluid retention. But not all gains or losses are important. For

' I had antenatal care at my GP's antenatal clinic and got to know Jane, my midwife, so well that she became a friend. Thinking about tests is the worst part of pregnancy, but she discussed it until I felt ready to make a decision. She listens to the baby's heart with an ear trumpet and the first time she heard it she stuck a stethoscope on the end so that I could hear it too. I don't know which of us was more excited.

Going for check-ups made me feel special because of Jane's attitude. I could ask anything without feeling silly. I don't have anyone to share the excitement of pregnancy with; luckily Jane seemed as interested in every little detail as I was. ' ALISON

ANTENATAL CHECKUPS

◆ *Take your partner, a friend or a book to your first antenatal visit –
you may have to wait between examinations.*

◆ *Be open about any symptoms you have and ask questions about tests
or treatments suggested.*

◆ *If your blood pressure is high because of anxiety or stress ask if it can
be taken again in half an hour and use the time to consciously relax. This
will often bring it down to normal.*

instance, you might be wearing lighter or heavier clothes because the weather
has changed, or be laying down fat stores on your bottom or thighs, which are
normally used up while breastfeeding

A doctor will give you a physical examination to check your current state
of health. Internal examinations are less common today. Blood samples (see
below) will be taken and you may be asked to provide a mid-stream urine
sample (pass urine for a short time, then catch the sample in a supplied
container) to check for infection. An ultrasound scan or other special tests
(see page 56) will be offered.

At each antenatal visit your urine will be tested for sugar and protein,
possible signs of gestational diabetes (see page 53) and pre-eclampsia (see
page 102). Your blood pressure when your heart is pumping and at rest will
be taken using an inflated cuff around your upper arm. The midwife will also
feel your stomach to check the height of your uterus, and later your baby's
position. From about 18 weeks, or earlier with sophisticated equipment, she
will listen to your baby's heartbeat, and feel your ankles to test for any
swelling (see page 102).

Antenatal care should be considered a partnership between you and your
midwife. It's part of her job to give you unbiased information and help you
make informed decisions about what tests to have, where to have your baby
and so on. No examination or test is compulsory and the decisions are up to
you. At each visit you can ask for advice and discuss anything that worries or
interests you.

Routine blood tests

Blood samples are taken at your booking visit and later in pregnancy. The
analysis varies but includes checking for blood group and the rhesus factor
(see page 53) in case you need an emergency transfusion, plus tests for
glucose, syphilis, rubella and possibly hepatitis B. If you have no rubella antibodies you will be offered immunization after the birth. The other diseases
could harm your baby if left untreated. Some hospitals offer a full glucose
tolerance test on a separate occasion (see gestational diabetes, page 53). HIV

What your notes mean

If there is anything you don't understand it's better to ask than to go home and worry!
Here are some common phrases and abbreviations:

Your details:

Para 0/1/2 +1	You have had 0, 1 or 2 previous births. +1 means a miscarriage or termination before 28 weeks.
LB or SB	Live birth or stillbirth.
TCA 3/7 (4/52)	To come again in 3 days (or 4 weeks).
Brim	The inlet or upper rim of your pelvis.
Fundus	The top of your uterus, which rises in your stomach as your baby grows and descends a little when the baby's head engages (see below).
BP	Blood pressure.
PET	Pre-eclampsia (pre-eclamptic toxaemia) (see page 102).
US or USS	Ultrasound scan.

Urine:

NAD	Nothing abnormal discovered.
Alb/Tr Prot+ (or ++)	Albumin/trace of protein. The plus signs indicate the amount of protein found. This could signify the start of pre-eclampsia.
0 Gluc	No glucose found in the urine. Two per cent or more glucose would be considered high.

Blood:

Bloods	Blood tests done.
Hb	Haemoglobin or blood count.
Fe	Iron tablets. The prescription (e.g. Pregaday) may be recorded.
WR	Syphilis test VDRL/TPHA or FTA-Abs are alternatives.

The baby's health:

FMF or FMNF	Fetal movements felt, or not felt.
FH	Fetal heart. H or NH means heard or not heard. The heart rate (usually between 120 and 160 beats per minute) may be recorded.

The baby's position:

LOA/ROA	Left (or right) occiput anterior or LOP/ROP posterior (see page 105).
PP	Presenting part, or the part of your baby nearest to the cervix and likely to emerge first.
Vx or Ceph	Vertex or cephalic, meaning 'head down'.
Br/Tr	Breech (bottom down), or transverse (lying across the uterus).
Eng or E	Engaged. This refers to how far down your baby's head is in your pelvis. When recorded in fifths it means the proportion of your baby's head above the brim of your pelvis. So 1/5 means the head is almost fully engaged, ready for the birth, while 4/5 means it has started to engage.
NEng or NE	Not engaged.

tests are not routine or compulsory but may be carried out anonymously to monitor levels in the population. You would not be told your results.

Your haemoglobin level will be checked. Haemoglobin is the substance in red blood cells that carries oxygen around your body. The average blood count in pregnancy is about 12g. When you are anaemic (ie your haemoglobin level is too low) your heart has to work harder to supply your baby with oxygen, so you may be given iron tablets and folic acid supplements if your blood count is under about 10g.

Individual tests may be performed if you are at risk from a disease that needs special care in pregnancy, such as sickle cell anaemia, thalassaemia, toxoplasmosis (see page 18) or diabetes.

The rhesus factor: If a mother is rhesus negative and her partner, like 80 per cent of the population, is rhesus positive a problem may arise in future pregnancies if the baby inherits the father's blood group. The baby's blood will contain a D antigen and the mother's does not. If the baby's blood passes into the mother, as can happen during birth, miscarriage or termination, the mother's blood will form antibodies against the D antigen. These may attack the red blood cells of any future rhesus positive baby the mother carries.

If you are rhesus negative you will have extra blood tests to monitor your antibody status. Within three days of the birth you will be given an anti-D injection to destroy any cells from the baby's blood before antibodies are formed. About two per cent of women need treatment during pregnancy because the baby's blood cells have leaked across the placenta.

Blood pressure: Normal blood pressure is about 110/70. In pregnancy it varies, usually somewhere between 95/60 and 135/85. The systolic (upper) figure (measuring your heart when pumping) can be affected by stress, including anxiety or rushing to your appointment. The diastolic (lower) figure records your heart at rest. If it rises by 20 points above your normal baseline it could indicate pre-eclampsia (see page 102). The usual cut-off point for concern is 140/90, although in the absence of other symptoms there may be nothing to worry about.

High blood pressure can make you feel energetic just when you ought to be resting to help bring it down, while low blood pressure may make you feel faint or excessively tired. Although blood pressure outside the normal range is a potential problem during pregnancy, it is not your fault!

Gestational diabetes

Insulin regulates the glucose in your blood and eliminates any excess. To meet the needs of the baby, anti-insulin hormones in pregnancy allow extra glucose to circulate. If there is too much for the mother's and the baby's needs, the excess is excreted. About 50 per cent of pregnant women show traces of sugar in the urine at some stage, and more insulin is usually produced to compensate.

Women with gestational diabetes have high levels of sugar in their blood and urine because the anti-insulin hormones work so well that they cannot produce enough insulin, or cannot use the insulin they produce efficiently. This is rarely linked to 'ordinary' diabetes (inability to produce enough insulin when you are not pregnant), although treatments for the two conditions are similar, including a good diet and extra monitoring to keep your blood sugar at normal levels. With good care the risks to mother or baby from ordinary or gestational diabetes are much reduced.

Have you any questions?

At the end of your antenatal check you'll be asked if you have any questions. When you're pregnant for the first time it can be hard to think of any questions as you feel a complete novice. Later on you'll probably think of plenty of things to ask, but at your first visit there are things you might want to know, so that you don't miss out on something or find out about it too late. It is well worth writing down a list of questions to take along to your first antenatal appointment.

Ask where you could have your baby, to discover all the possibilities in your area. Some women get the impression that they have to go to a certain hospital, but this is not true. Before your visit you might like to look at the pros and cons of hospital, GP unit and home birth on page 84. You do not have to make your mind up immediately about where to have your baby but you can decide later when you have thought about it.

Ask what sort of antenatal care you can have. This is usually linked to where you have your baby. Look at the possibilities on page 27 and find out what happens in your area.

Finally, ask what tests are available to check that your baby is healthy. These are discussed on the next page. Some are carried out very early in pregnancy, or you might have to travel to a specialist centre to have them.

WHEN TO CONTACT YOUR DOCTOR

Even normal changes in pregnancy can be worrying when you first experience them. Here are the symptoms you should always report to your GP:

◆ *Vaginal bleeding – it may be no problem, but it's best to check.*

◆ *Abdominal pain or cramps that get increasingly severe.*

◆ *High temperature, fever symptoms or excessive vomiting.*

◆ *Severe headache that doesn't respond to the usual remedies, blurred vision, or swelling of your feet so that you can't get your shoes on. These could indicate pre-eclampsia (see page 102).*

◆ *Any other symptom that worries you.*

WILL MY BABY BE ALRIGHT?

Anxiety about whether your baby will be perfect is natural. About 4 per cent of liveborn babies have an abnormality. No one knows what causes most of these, but more than half of them are either mild, such as an extra toe or a birthmark, or moderate such as a cleft palate or congenital dislocation of the hip. They may need no treatment or an operation (sometimes very minor), and the baby will lead a normal life.

Older mothers often worry that they are at greater risk of having a child with a disability than younger mothers, but only chromosomal abnormalities increase with age. For example, there is a one in 800 chance of having a baby with a major chromosomal abnormality at age 30. At age 35 it's one in 335, at 40 it's one in 100 and at 45 it's one in 25.

Testing for fetal abnormalities is part of antenatal care. If you feel that a termination is preferable to bringing a disabled baby into the world they offer this choice. They may also offer reassurance so that you can enjoy the rest of your pregnancy.

But tests have disadvantages: they are not totally accurate, they only detect certain problems (for example, most rare single gene defects are not detectable at present), and they cannot show the degree of disability which may vary considerably.

If you are not particularly worried, think carefully before having a test just because it's available. Some hospitals offer tests with the expectation that if an abnormality is diagnosed you will want a termination, but not all women agree with this. It's better to clarify your feelings in advance rather than jump on a roundabout that may be difficult to get off.

Most women will be reassured by their results. Those who are not face difficult choices: to have more tests, to continue pregnancy knowing their baby may have a problem, or to opt for termination. Such decisions are never easy to make.

Special tests

Broadly speaking, invasive tests like amniocentesis, chorionic villus sampling (CVS) and cordocentesis carry small risks but they do diagnose with a good measure of certainty the presence of chromosomal, genetic and metabolic defects. Procedures such as ultrasound scans and blood tests that do not involve penetrating the uterus carry fewer risks to the baby, but give less information.

Hospitals protocols regarding how and when tests are performed vary. Most women are offered an ultrasound scan, although routine scans do not always check for abnormalities. In some areas women over 35 or with a family history of a handicap are offered amniocentesis. In others, all women are offered a blood test followed by amniocentesis if the results suggest that the baby might have a handicap. If a test is not available locally you could arrange referral to a centre that provides it. If you are considered low risk a test may only be offered privately.

The more experienced a hospital is at providing tests and interpreting results the better. Recently introduced tests may be less reliable and carry more risks. Ask your doctor for up-to-date local information.

Blood tests select pregnancies where the baby may be at higher risk of certain defects so that the mother can be offered further tests. The AFP test analyses alphafetoprotein levels to assess the risk of neural tube defects such as spina bifida. The triple and triple-plus tests combine various markers with your age to give a predicted risk for neural tube defects and chromosome abnormalities such as Down's syndrome.

The triple-plus test is performed from 13 weeks; others from about 15-22 weeks. Results are available in a week or two. Ten per cent of women score below one in 250 and will be offered amniocentesis.

Blood tests can cause unnecessary anxiety. They are not very reliable – 60 per cent (triple) and about 80 per cent (triple-plus). Only 10 per cent of women with raised AFP levels will be carrying a baby with a defect.

Ultrasound scans: Scans can date a pregnancy fairly accurately at 16-18 weeks (see page 62), check your baby's growth, diagnose multiple pregnancies and establish the position of your baby or placenta. They detect abnormalities in the spine and organs such as the heart or kidneys, although before 13 weeks most scans only pick up major defects. They cannot detect genetic, metabolic or chromosomal abnormalities unless there are physical signs associated with them.

The best time for anomaly screening is 18-22 weeks, or 30-plus weeks for minor defects. A scan's effectiveness at detecting defects depends on the quality of the equipment, the skill of the technician, your baby's position and the time taken over the procedure.

‘ *I enjoyed my antenatal care, apart from waiting around at my first visit to the hospital. I wanted my baby to be healthy so I took all the advice offered, but of course I had moments of wondering what I'd do if she wasn't!*

I decided not to have tests after talking to my partner, my GP and friends who'd had them. I didn't think the evidence would tell me enough to base a decision on, and felt that I wouldn't be given anything I couldn't cope with. That was more important than numbers on a bit of paper saying I was low risk or whatever. ’ JOANNE

Before a scan you drink plenty of water, as a full bladder pushes the uterus forward to give a better picture. Your abdomen is lubricated with gel and a transducer bounces high frequency waves off your baby to build up a picture on a TV screen. It's exciting to see your baby and can help you feel close to her. But although scans appear to be safe nobody knows if there are long-term risks to future generations. Some people feel they should not be used routinely. If you are uncertain, ask the reason for the scan.

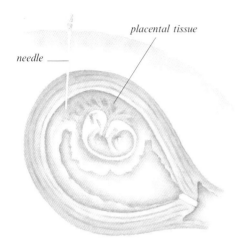

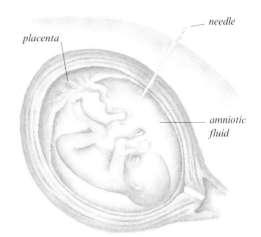

Above: *Chorionic Villus Sampling (CVS).*
Cells are taken from the edge of the placenta
at about 10-14 weeks.
Above right: *Amniocentesis. A sample of*
amniotic fluid is withdrawn at about 16-18
weeks.
Right: *Cordocentesis. A sample of the baby*
blood is withdrawn from near the placenta
after 18 weeks.

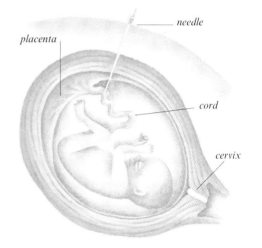

Amniocentesis: Amniocentesis is performed at about 16 to 18 weeks to detect abnormalities such as Down's syndrome, cystic fibrosis and Tay Sach's disease. Guided by a scan, a fine, hollow needle is passed through your abdomen and a sample of amniotic fluid is taken from around your baby. Cells are cultured so results take three to five weeks to come through. You may wish to ask your baby's sex; if you're told it's a girl there is a slight chance that the female cells cultured could be yours, not your baby's.

Occasionally amniocentesis causes infection. There is a one per cent risk of miscarriage and a one per cent risk that the test will need to be repeated, with the same risk of miscarriage. Three per cent of babies have breathing problems after birth, but these are usually temporary and mild.

Chorionic villus sampling (CVS): This detects similar abnormalities to amniocentesis. A sample of the chorionic villi (the tissue that will later develop into the placenta) is taken through the vagina or the abdomen at

'*If you decide to have tests you need to talk it through with your partner so that you're both sure what you would do if there was a problem. Our experience ended happily with the birth of a perfect baby, but my pregnancy was stressful.*

My triple test suggested a risk of Down's syndrome so I had an amniocentesis. This showed an abnormality and I went to London for cordocentesis. Although we were given the all clear my husband and I were still afraid that something was wrong. We didn't admit it to each other until afterwards, but I couldn't look forward to the birth in case something happened. ' ANNETTE

about 10-12 weeks. Results take a few days. There may be at least one per cent risk of miscarriage, up to two per cent risk of false positive results (changes in the cells of the chorionic villi that are not present in your baby), and one per cent chance that the test may need repeating. Recently there have been concerns about the test affecting the baby. The skills of the laboratory technician and the doctor who carries out the test are significant in maximizing reliability and safety. A doctor needs to perform about 75 tests to learn the technique.

Cordocentesis (Fetal blood sampling): Cordocentesis tests for a wide range of defects plus diseases such as rubella and toxoplasmosis. A needle is inserted through your abdomen into the umbilical vein in the cord close to the placenta, and a sample of blood is withdrawn. It is performed after 18 weeks when the baby's blood vessels are big enough.

It is not widely available and is only done to confirm a diagnosis suspected after other tests. The results are available in about two days, depending on the problem. The miscarriage risk is two to four per cent, or less if the doctor performs over 30 tests a year.

Early tests

Specialist centres are developing early tests. Contact your Regional Health Information Service or WellBeing (see Appendix) for details. Early scans will be offered in some regional hospitals from 1995. You would have to travel to the centre for other tests. Some are still under evaluation and they may carry greater risks. However, reassurance or termination if necessary is available sooner in pregnancy. For many women this is an important advantage.

First Trimester Scan: Using high-quality equipment at between 11 and 13 weeks it's possible to measure a dark space behind the baby's neck. If this space is 3mm or more the risk that the baby has a chromosomal abnormality is at least five times higher than your age alone would predict and you will be offered CVS or amniocentesis. If it is less than 3mm the risk is six to seven times less than that of any woman of your age and you might feel sufficiently reassured not to have an invasive test carrying the risk of miscarriage. Women with normal or reduced risks are usually advised to have an anomaly scan at about 20 weeks to exclude defects not linked with chromosomal abnormalities.

Coelocentesis: This involves testing the coelomic fluid around the amniotic sac for chromosomal defects. It can be performed before 10 weeks and may carry less risk of miscarriage than CVS.

Deciding about tests

Fetal testing produces dilemmas that previous generations never had to face. The burden of responsibility may feel impossibly heavy to bear when you realize that the tests themselves carry potential risks as well as benefits, and the decisions are down to you.

Whether you opt for testing depends on how you weigh up the risks and benefits. For instance, at the age of 40 the risks of amniocentesis causing a miscarriage or detecting a major chromosomal defect are equal: one in a hundred. If you are under 40 years of age the risk of miscarriage is greater than the likelihood of detecting a problem. If you're over 40 years old it's the other way round.

You might also want to consider factors such as how easily you conceive, how important *this* baby is to you and how you feel about having an affected child. If you were 38 years old and worried about having a baby with Down's syndrome, detecting this might outweigh the risk of a miscarriage. On the other hand, a woman of 42 who had trouble conceiving and has fewer chances of conceiving again might feel the risk of losing a baby through an invasive test is too high.

Many people with a disability are saddened by the fear their condition arouses in others. But fear is not always rational. It depends on your view of the world, your emotional and financial resources, your experience of children with a disability and the effects you feel such a child would have on you and your family.

Some reasons for having tests:
- You simply could not cope with a handicapped baby. Tests may reassure you or give you the option of termination.
- You already have a child with a disability or a family history of a defect, and want to know if this baby is affected.
- You feel that having tests means you have done everything possible to avoid having a child with a disability.
- You feel the potential drawbacks are a small price to pay for the information or reassurance tests could provide.

Some reasons for not having tests:
- You feel that they would not give you accurate enough information on which to base decisions.
- You are not unduly anxious and want to enjoy your pregnancy without the worry tests might cause.
- You prefer to accept what comes and would find out about a disability and cope if it happened.

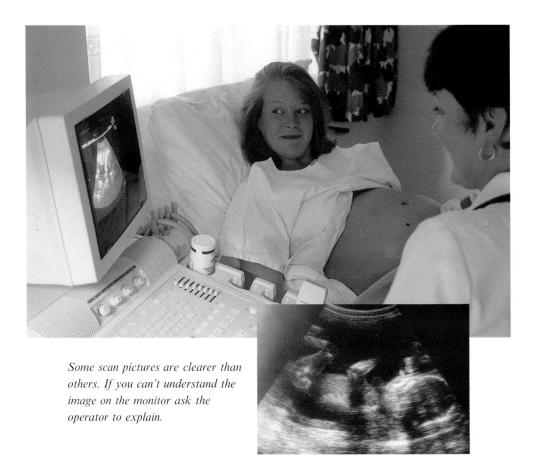

Some scan pictures are clearer than others. If you can't understand the image on the monitor ask the operator to explain.

The following summary may help you decide, with your family and your doctor, the test that is right for you.

Blood test: Blood tests carry no risks but they may increase anxiety. Ten per cent of women are offered amniocentesis, so think twice if you don't want to risk an invasive test. If you are considered high risk but want to avoid amniocentesis a blood test might reassure you. If you are not offered a blood test you could ask to pay privately. The triple-plus test is more reliable than the triple test.

Amniocentesis: If you want a definite diagnosis waiting for blood test results would delay this, so consider going straight for amniocentesis.

CVS: An option if you want a definite diagnosis early in pregnancy and a centre near you offers it.

Ultrasound scans: Brief routine scans do not check for all physical defects, but an anomaly scan at 20 weeks might reassure you. A first trimester scan to measure the dark space behind the baby's neck might help you decide whether to have further tests.

Waiting for results

Waiting for results may be more stressful than you anticipate. Wondering if your baby has a defect brings unexpected and distressing emotions, and if further tests are suggested most women expect the worst so waiting is especially stressful. You never think you'll face this situation so it's always a shock, and your confidence may be so shaken that you never feel completely reassured until your baby is born.

Remember that more than half the women who are offered further tests will be told that all is well; and that around half of all abnormalities are mild or moderate defects that can be treated.

Facing an adverse result: Many women intend to have a termination if there's a problem, but what seemed the obvious choice when there was a strong possibility it would not be necessary can be much harder when your pregnancy is showing and you can feel your baby moving.

You may worry about ending a pregnancy needlessly because the test was wrong, or the baby was only mildly affected. This is something you will never know so it's best to assume the test is correct. Termination is not, of course, the only option. You could continue your pregnancy even though your baby might not live or might be disabled. Another possibility you could consider is fostering or adoption.

Don't be pressured into making quick judgements; thinking about things for a few days will make little difference. The decision has to be one that you can live with. It isn't easy and you will need support.

Discuss the results with your GP or a genetic specialist, and your family. It may help to talk to parents who have faced similar decisions, or to someone with the same disability. Organizations that can put you in touch with someone, give you information or support you whatever your decision are listed in the Appendix.

Coping with termination: Although it is distressing to think about it, knowing what may happen can make termination less daunting. You will be admitted to the gynaecology or maternity ward, and will probably be given a single room. If the pregnancy is less than 14 weeks, the neck of the uterus is usually dilated and the fetus is removed under general anaesthetic. Between 14 and 18 weeks obstetricians have different policies, some favouring dilatation and evacuation and others feeling that induced labour is safer.

After 18 weeks it is considered safer to induce labour using prostaglandin pessaries or a drip (see page 146). Because the uterus is not ready for labour it can be longer and more painful, but your partner or a friend can be with you and pain relief will be available. The thought of going through labour may be profoundly upsetting, but this really is safer for you.

Termination inevitably causes great sadness. It's hard to take such a responsibility, but uncertainty is part of life and you can only make a decision with the knowledge you have at the time. If you have done your best you have to assume your choice was the right one. Discuss how you feel with a good listener. Your midwife or a sympathetic friend may help if your partner feels unable to talk about it because of his own distress.

Give yourself time to come to terms with feelings of grief or guilt. Emotional pain cannot be anaesthetized; it has to be faced and lived through. Taking positive steps to come to terms with it will help you to move forward more confidently to a new pregnancy.

QUESTIONS AND ANSWERS

Q: Going by my last period, my baby is due on 17 May. A scan at 12 weeks said I am due on 22 May but another at 20 weeks gave 14 May as my due date. A midwife said they judge when a baby is due from the scan dates, but which ones?

A: Scans date a pregnancy accurately to within a few days at 7-12 weeks. From 13-20 weeks they are slightly less accurate (within a week) and after 20 weeks they are steadily less reliable. The earlier scan date is probably the one to go on. Your baby is likely to arrive within a week either side of May 22. Having said this, babies sometimes ignore what they are supposed to do and arrive when they feel like it!

Q: When I was scanned at 14 weeks I was told that my placenta is low and I'll need another scan later on to see if it has moved. If not I may need a Caesarean section. Why is this?

A: Usually the placenta implants in the upper wall, well out of the way of the cervix, or neck of the uterus. If it was low down it might begin to detach when the cervix opens. Depending on the degree, a Caesarean section might be the safest option. A placenta that lies completely over the cervix (*placenta praevia*) would prevent the baby from emerging safely, so a Caesarean birth would certainly be planned.

The placenta doesn't physically change position, but early in pregnancy it's hard to tell if it has implanted in the lower area of the uterus or what will become the upper part. This can be checked by another scan later on, when the uterus is bigger. The majority are found to be absolutely fine.

Q: I'm three months pregnant and my doctor says I've put on half the total weight gain I'm allowed already. Should I go on a diet?

A: In early pregnancy women who suffer nausea and vomiting sometimes put on no weight. Others gain weight rapidly, laying down fat stores on thighs and buttocks that are used up when breastfeeding. Doctors often suggest a total gain of 25-45lb (11-20kg) is reasonable. A large-framed woman would be towards the upper end and a petite woman at the lower end.

These are guidelines and there are wide variations. Excess weight increases the risk of minor problems such as varicose veins and backache and may contribute to more serious problems.

The quality of the food you eat is probably more important than the quantity. Eat according to your appetite, and no more. Don't diet, except on medical advice, as using up your fat stores would only provide your baby with calories and babies also need a steady supply of nutrients to grow healthily.

Q: My sister prevented stretch marks by rubbing oil into her stomach every day, but a friend who also did so said it made no difference. What should I do?

A: Stretch marks appear on your stomach, thighs or breasts. They look like purplish streaks under the skin and are caused by the lower layers stretching. Women who gain weight rapidly tend to have more of them but it also depends on skin type. Rubbing in oil or special creams doesn't prevent them, although it may make your skin feel more comfortable. If your sister has no stretch marks you may have inherited skin with good elasticity. About 90 per cent of women develop at least a few. and some women get a lot. Occasionally a rash develops, but your GP can prescribe something for it. Stretch marks gradually fade to cream or silvery grey. Look on them as a badge of motherhood!

Q: I have a small frame and my midwife says my baby is a good size. I'm worried about having a difficult birth. Should I eat less so that the baby will be smaller?

A: When your midwife says your baby is a 'good size' she may mean exactly right for you, or she may simply be making conversation! It can be remarkably hard to judge a baby's size before birth. Anxiety often makes women give doctors' and midwives' pronouncements unjustified significance.

The sort of birth you have depends on the size of your pelvic cavity (not your overall frame so don't worry about your height or shoe size), the amount of the hormone relaxin circulating to increase its dimensions, and the position of the baby. A small woman with a good-sized pelvic cavity or plenty of relaxin circulating could give birth to a big baby more easily than a large woman whose baby was in an awkward position.

Try to eat nutritious food according to your appetite as a healthy mother is more likely to have a normal birth. If you eat slightly less than your body requires your own health will suffer as your baby is served first; if you eat much less your baby will fail to grow. This is undesirable and could make the birth more complicated rather than easier.

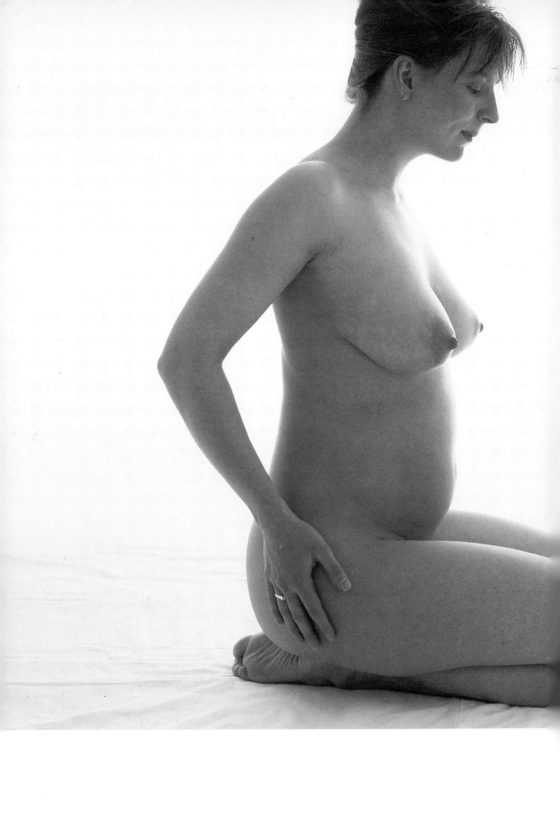

5

Mid-Pregnancy

(MONTHS 4–6)

' I felt my baby flutter today!
Suddenly I'm alive and full of energy.
Everywhere the world seems filled with
pregnant bumps. I never really noticed
how many there are around before
I had one myself! '

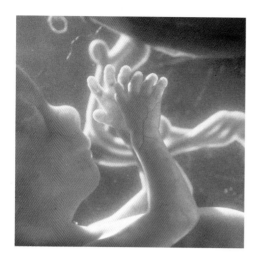

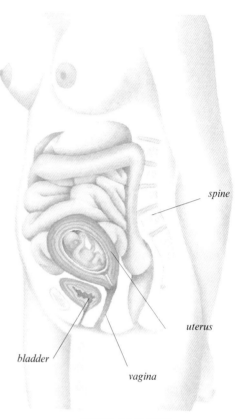

spine

uterus

bladder

vagina

FOUR MONTHS

Above: *This fetus is about four months. You can see the umbilical cord by the hands.*
Right: *Fourth month: Your uterus has expanded into your abdominal cavity and soon you'll feel the baby's movements.*
Fifth month: There's less room for your intestines and stomach as your uterus takes up the space.
Sixth month: Your baby still has room to turn somersaults in your uterus.

HOW YOUR BABY DEVELOPS

In the fourth month your baby and the placenta are each about the length of your first finger. 'Placenta' means cake in Latin, reflecting both its shape and its nourishing function.

The blood vessels in the umbilical cord carry food and waste products between you and your baby. Their walls are like a mesh fence, excluding large molecules while allowing small molecules and gases to filter through. So anaesthetics and some infections can pass from mother to baby and certain drugs can be used to treat the baby via the mother. Like a water-filled garden hose the cord rarely becomes knotted as it uncurls if the baby's movements tangle it.

By 16 weeks your baby is as long as your hand and as heavy as an apple. He floats in about a teacupful of amniotic fluid. His eyes, ears and nose are well formed and his fingernails and genitals can now be identified. At the end of the fifth month he measures about 12in (30cm) and weighs 1lb (450g). Now

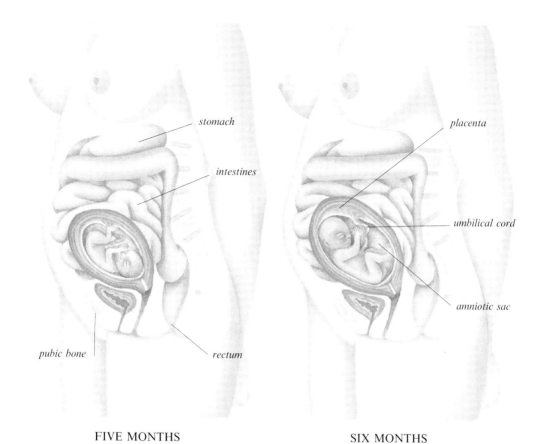

FIVE MONTHS   SIX MONTHS

he has eyelashes and pale pink nipples and the buds of his permanent teeth are forming. Your baby opens his eyes and looks around. His grip develops and he makes breathing movements with his chest. Although still too imma-ture to function on his own, all his bodily systems are beginning to work.

HOW YOU MAY FEEL

By about 16 weeks the exhaustion, sickness and see-saw emotions you may have been experiencing usually settle down. It's a great morale booster to feel pregnant rather than ill! A first pregnancy often barely shows for five or six months, but with later pregnancies you may lose your waist by the fourth month. Most women enjoy looking pregnant, but some are mildly embar-rassed or feel that instead of looking pregnant they simply look fat!

For the next few weeks you may feel relaxed and fulfilled, although you could also experience apprehension about the future, and a feeling that you

COMMON MID-PREGNANCY SYMPTOMS

◆ *Hair and skin problems similar to those experienced before a period, caused by increased secretion of oils.*

◆ *Red, itchy patches or dark pigmentation on your skin, brittle nails, or a heightened sense of smell.*

◆ *An ache at one or both sides of your abdomen, caused by the fibrous ligaments that anchor the uterus in your body stretching as your baby grows.*

◆ *Increased vaginal secretions and a tendency to overheat more easily because of the extra blood circulating.*

◆ *Vivid dreams as your sleep is disturbed by your baby's movements and you wake up more frequently.*

cannot quite keep your usual grip on life! Fortunately, these moments of self-doubt often occur between periods when you feel utterly confident and almost euphoric.

Many women feel and look healthy, with thicker hair and a clear skin, but others wonder when the flower of womanhood will start to bloom! As the growing uterus takes up space in your abdomen, moving your intestines and stomach aside to make room, you may begin to experience annoying discomforts. If they are troublesome talk to your doctor or try a self-help remedy (see page 72). The symptoms listed at the top of this page usually disappear soon after the birth.

RELATIONSHIP WITH YOUR PARTNER

Your partner also has to adjust to parenthood, which will affect him as profoundly as it affects you. As your pregnancy progresses he may become more actively involved, encouraging your efforts to get fit, or helping to gather information and make decisions about the birth. He may re-think his attitude to work or life in general, make changes in his commitments, notice small jobs around the home that have been ignored for months, or enthusiastically decide that you should move house before the birth.

However, some men react by withdrawing to ground where they feel more confident; for example, taking on extra work or spending more time with their friends. If your partner resists taking an active interest don't pressure him. He may change his mind in time.

Pregnancy is a time of transition for both partners but, while you have your expanding girth to focus attention on you, your partner has no physical signs to mark him out in any way. It's easy to overlook his needs, especially if like many men he finds it hard to talk about feelings.

About one man in 10 suffers mild anxiety symptoms, such as toothache, stomach ache, loss of appetite or sickness. This is called the 'couvade' and in some cultures it is expected and ritualized because it re-focuses attention towards the father and helps him to handle change. Many fathers become less anxious as the pregnancy advances and they begin to adjust to their new role.

Making love

Some couples want to make love more often during pregnancy and others find their libido declines. The most common experience is that sexual desire fluctuates, often increasing in mid-pregnancy and declining nearer the birth. You may be more aware of your sexuality during the fifth and sixth months, when your blood supply and vaginal secretions are increased. Enthusiasm is catching and can lead to a more satisfying sex life than ever. The physical and emotional changes of pregnancy affect desire and pleasure positively and negatively. Body image can be a real issue for some couples. Some women dislike having a rounded body and need reassurance that they are still attractive. Some men find the voluptuous shapes and stronger smells of pregnancy turn them off. Equally, many couples find these factors a novel delight.

Your partner may become anxious about the baby, but intercourse that is comfortable and enjoyable for you is not harmful, although you may need to choose positions that do not cause pressure on your abdomen or deep penetration. If your pregnancy is unstable your doctor might suggest abstention. Orgasm may cause colostrum (a creamy substance) to leak from your breasts, or mild, harmless contractions, but it does not normally cause miscarriage or premature labour. Oral sex is safe and can be a substitute for intercourse if you both find it enjoyable.

The quality of a relationship is built not on prowess in bed but on communication, love and understanding. Your sexual needs and your partner's may alter as pregnancy progresses. Be patient and talk about any difficulties. You will find that making these adjustments infinitely strengthens your love life.

FEELING THE BABY MOVE

For most women, feeling the baby move for the first time is a red letter day. It can happen any time between about 14 and 25 weeks. Babies are particularly active between 24 and 28 weeks. Later, they have distinct periods of rest and activity and the kicks feel stronger, a daily reminder that they are fine. If you have not felt movement for a while try sending a 'thought message' to your baby – you may get a reassuring kick in reply. A series of rhythmic knocks means your baby has hiccups!

Typically, women begin to feel movements at about 18 weeks for a first baby and somewhat earlier for subsequent babies, but they describe the sensation of those first kicks differently:

'It felt soft and fluttery, like a butterfly kiss on your cheek. I wasn't sure if I was imagining it at first.'

'I thought a fly had landed on my tummy. When I looked there was nothing there, but I felt it again and knew immediately what it was.'

'It was like somebody knocking or bumping against my stomach but from the inside. It became more definite over a week or two.'

'The nearest I can describe it is a rolling or lurching sensation. I thought it was wind at first!'

Getting to know your baby

You may think that bonding is something that only happens after the birth, but for most women the process starts long before this. Thinking about your baby's welfare, worrying that he will be alright, or imagining your future life together is evidence of the bond between you.

Finding out about your baby's likes and dislikes can be great fun. He may respond to certain types of music, or to his father's voice. He may stop kicking when you massage your abdomen, sing to him or sway your body; or he may decide that it's playtime as soon as you sit or lie down!

When he's in the mood he may play 'games' with you, pushing your hand away when you gently press the bulge of a foot or a hand. The more you get to know your baby before he's born the more familiar he will feel when you hold him in your arms.

STAYING WELL

Considering the changes your body undergoes in pregnancy a certain amount of discomfort is to be expected. Doctors rarely treat common symptoms such as cramp and backache unless they are extremely troublesome, because they are caused by the very things that help to maintain a healthy pregnancy – your hormones, extra blood supply and increasing weight. This doesn't mean that you have to suffer silently. Many minor problems can be avoided by common sense or alleviated by self-help remedies.

Remember to look after your body! Get some fresh air and exercise every day and make sufficient rest a priority. Eat regularly and drink plenty of fluids. These simple measures will help you to cope with the extra demands of pregnancy and may prevent a range of symptoms, from mild headaches to backache and constipation. If you still have a problem, check with your GP that it's nothing serious, then try a self-help remedy or alternative therapy.

' Feeling movements makes up for everything else in pregnancy. At first I thought of the baby as a fish-like creature, but now I think of her as a little person. I feel very protective and grateful for each kick as I know she's alright. She won't kick for my partner, though. As soon as he puts his hand on my tummy she goes quite still and quiet! ' DEE

Massage Techniques
Sit or kneel while your partner massages your shoulders. He presses his thumbs on either side of your spine, working in small circles around the line of your shoulder blades.

Alternatively, lie on your back, resting your head in your partner's lap while he sits or kneels. He gently strokes along your jaw, your cheeks and your forehead.

You could also kneel or lie on your side while your partner slowly and firmly strokes his palms down your back, hand over hand. This can be comforting in early labour.

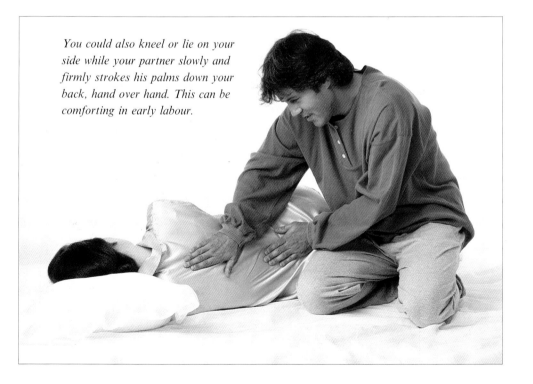

How to help yourself

Try the following self-help remedies for these common pregnancy problems:

Cramp: Painful muscle spasm, often in your leg or foot.

Self-help: Pull your foot upwards instead of pointing your toes when you stretch on waking up. To improve your circulation, roll an empty milk bottle vigorously under your bare foot every night before going to bed. Aromatherapy massage may help. Try increasing your intake of calcium, (in milk and cheese, for example) or cut down if you eat a lot of any food, such as dairy produce or bananas.

Fainting: Feeling light headed or dizzy may be caused by lowered blood pressure or low blood sugar levels.

Self-help: Lie on your side or prop yourself up with pillows (see page 101). Keep a healthy snack handy to maintain your blood sugar levels. Dress in layers and carry a battery fan, mineral water or a spray to refresh yourself. To forestall dizziness, press down on the balls of your feet – the guardsman's trick. If you feel faint sit with your head between your knees or lie down.

Varicose veins: Soft, blue knotted cords in the legs, caused by extra blood passing through veins with relaxed walls.

Self-help: Put your feet up whenever possible, but shift your weight from foot to foot if you have to stand. Avoid crossing your legs, sitting on a hard chair edge, wearing tight knicker elastic, knee highs or hold-up stockings. Keep support tights under your pillow and put them on before getting up. If you forget, raise your legs and hips for ten minutes to drain blood towards your heart before putting them on.

Constipation: Hormones and your growing uterus slow down the passage of waste from the body.

Self-help: Drink more fluids and eat more fruit, vegetables or fibre-rich foods such as bran or oats. Prune juice or dried prunes are natural laxatives. If iron tablets make you constipated ask your GP to prescribe a different brand. Always go to the toilet when you need to – raise your feet on a stool or upturned bucket and relax your pelvic floor (see page 45).

Piles (haemorrhoids): Swollen veins in the rectum or around the anus, that may bleed or be itchy and painful.

Self-help: Avoid straining on the toilet. Drink plenty of fluids and do pelvic floor exercises (see page 45) to improve your blood circulation. Avoid hot baths which make the blood vessels dilate; warm baths may be soothing. Ice packs, a proprietary cream or a pad soaked in witch hazel lotion from the chemist may give temporary relief. Increasing your intake of vitamins C, E and B6 may help.

Stress incontinence: When you cough or laugh you 'leak' some urine, or you need to go to the toilet when your bladder is empty.

Self-help: Do pelvic floor exercises (see page 45). Never try to hold on if you know your bladder is full. If you feel the urge when you know your bladder is empty gently tighten your pelvic floor and fix your mind on something else until the sensation subsides – in a few days things should improve.

Heartburn: A burning pain in your chest, or a sour taste in your mouth. Pressure on the relaxed stomach valve allows acid from partly digested food to 'burn' your oesophagus.

Self-help: Eat little and often, drink separately so that your stomach is not too full, and avoid spicy and fatty foods. At the first sign of heartburn, take something alkaline such as a sip of milk to neutralize the acid in your oesophagus and prevent a sore patch developing. Don't exercise or bend before a meal has had time to be digested. Raise your head and shoulders on pillows in bed. Ask your GP or pharmacist for an antacid preparation.

Itchiness: Your skin may itch, especially in the stomach area, because bile salts are not metabolized so well during pregnancy.

Self-help: Drink plenty of water to help flush out your system. Calamine lotion or half a cupful of bicarbonate of soda in a warm bath may soothe itching. Use aqueous cream or emulsifying ointment (from the chemist) instead of soap which can be drying.

Alternative therapies

These can be helpful to treat pregnancy discomforts and make you feel good. Some of them can be harmful during pregnancy so it's very important that you only go to a qualified practitioner. Your Regional Health Information Service (see Appendix) can advise you. Declare your pregnancy from the start even if you think it's obvious! Here are some therapies:

Acupuncture: Fine sterile needles are inserted at certain points to balance the flow of energy in the body. This can stimulate your body to produce endorphins (pain relieving substances), and help relieve problems such as nausea or fluid retention.

Aromatherapy: Essential oils or plant extracts are massaged into the body. Treatment may seem to be a pleasantly scented massage that gives a feeling of well-being, but it can affect your nervous system and hormones. To be safe, only consult someone who is fully qualified.

Homeopathy: Based on the principle 'like treats like', minute amounts of substances that produce the symptom are given, to stimulate the body's own defences. It can alleviate nausea and digestive problems for example, and also prepare your body for the birth and help speed recovery.

Medical Herbalism: This ancient healing art uses the entire leaf, bark or root of a plant instead of extracting an active ingredient from it. It's gentle, but treatments can be just as powerful as conventional drugs and need similar caution. Morning sickness and anaemia often respond well.

Osteopathy: A widely accepted therapy that treats skeletal and muscle problems using leverage and manipulation. There is a special clinic (see Appendix) to treat problems in pregnancy.

Exercise in pregnancy

Good circulation and suppleness will make pregnancy more comfortable. Any form of exercise that helps develop stamina and suppleness is beneficial. For example, you could swim regularly, or combine exercise, fresh air and recreation by taking a brisk walk for half an hour two or three times a week.

These stretching exercises make you more aware of your body and reduce stiffness. Hormone-softened ligaments can be overstrained, so warm up gently first and stretch slowly, holding a pose for a few seconds up to a few minutes. Repeat each exercise about six times, and do not overdo things.

Some exercises can be adapted; for example, if you get uncomfortable or lightheaded lying on the floor do the exercise on page 77 standing against a wall: with your knees bent, tighten your abdominal muscles and pull your back firmly against the wall, holding it for a few seconds.

Above: Inner Thighs

Sit for a few minutes each day with your back straight and the soles of your feet together. Rest your forearms on your knees and let them relax downwards without forcing or bouncing them.

Left: Back and Thighs

Sit with your back straight and legs apart. Lean gently forwards, pushing your heels away. Feel your back, thighs and calves stretch. Relax and rotate your ankles to improve your circulation.

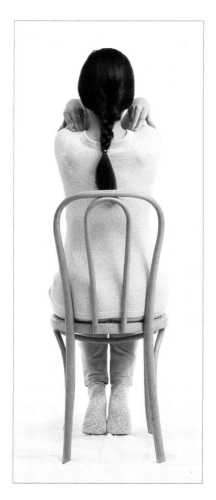

Right and below:
Neck and Upper Back
Sit up straight with your
hands on your shoulders.
Sweep your elbows
round in wide circles.
Feel the stretch
loosening any stiffness.

It's worth doing upper
body exercises such as
these if you use a
wheelchair. You may be
able to adapt other
exercises from a book
or ask a physiotherapist
for advice.

EXERCISE IN PREGNANCY

◆ *If you have any doubts about suitable exercise ask your GP's advice.*

◆ *Join a pregnancy exercise class where you'll meet other mums-to-be and may form friendships to enjoy after your baby is born. Ask at your local health club, leisure centre, swimming pool, hospital or health clinic.*

◆ *If you have a disability talk to the class teacher first to make sure that the location is suitable and she can provide appropriate exercises.*

◆ *If you join a general exercise class make sure the instructor knows that you are pregnant and can advise you.*

◆ *Be wary of taking up a new sport in pregnancy, and of any competitive sports or activities that could prevent you from listening to your own body.*

◆ *Stop any exercise that 'feels wrong', hurts, or leaves you exhausted rather than refreshed.*

Pelvic Rock
Right: *Stand with your feet apart and your knees slightly bent. Tighten your buttock muscles and tuck your 'tail' under.*

Far right: *Release your buttocks and swing your pelvis gently back with your body upright and your knees in the same position throughout.*

Rock your pelvis back and forth to loosen it and help prevent backache. When you feel comfortable with this, move your pelvis from side to side like a belly dancer (not illustrated).

Abdominal Exercise *(see page 74)*
*1. Lie on the floor with your arms a
little way from your body and your
knees hip width apart and bent.*

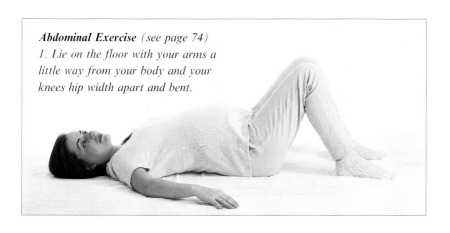

*2. Flatten your back to the floor –
notice the difference between
pictures 1 and 2.*

*3. Very slowly slide your feet along the
floor while keeping your back pressed
firmly down. As soon as it begins to
arch bend your knees and try again.*

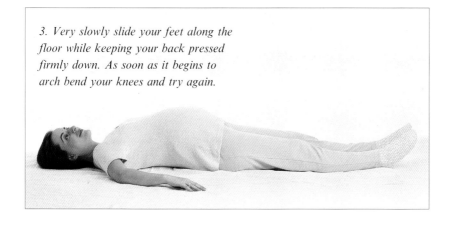

PREGNANCY AND WORK

In mid-pregnancy you usually have more energy, so working is easier; but it's still tiring, so don't expect too much of yourself. Most women stop work when maternity pay and leave become available about 11 weeks before the baby is due. Depending on certain regulations, your health and the demands of your job, you may want to stop sooner. If you want to work for longer your employer may require a letter from your doctor saying that you are fit.

You may count the days until you can stop work, or you may dread leaving. Either way, most women have mixed feelings when they stop work. While you are adjusting to life as a lady of leisure, take time to make friends in your neighbourhood. It can be harder to make the effort after the birth.

A good balance between work, recreation and rest will help you to enjoy your pregnancy. Try these tips:

- Conserve energy whenever you can and use every spare moment to consciously relax. Don't rush around in your lunch hour. Instead, try resting at your desk or in the car, or put your feet up in your firm's rest room.
- Put your social life on 'slow' for a bit and get regular early nights.
- Rearrange your work hours to avoid travel during rush hour. Ask politely for a seat on public transport.
- Don't leave things like decorating the nursery too late. You may not feel energetic by the time you get maternity leave.

MATERNITY CLOTHES

The golden rule for maternity wear is comfort, so avoid tight waistbands, skirts that ride up or very high heels that throw your pelvis out of balance and cause backache.

If you are too large for your regular clothes but feel awkward wearing maternity clothes, raid your partner's wardrobe for bigger shirts and sweaters, or buy clothes a size or two larger than usual that you can wear later on. You will not be your normal size for several weeks after the birth but most women do not want to continue wearing maternity clothes.

'I'm used to being active and it's frustrating not being able to do as much as usual. I run out of steam in the afternoon so at lunch time I lie down in the company medical room.

My husband and I have our main meal in the canteen so that we don't have to cook in the evening. We have salad or put a pizza under the grill for supper and I eat with my feet up in front of the TV. It gives me a real boost of energy. ' SALLY

In the past there has been a lack of smart, affordable business clothes but this problem has been tackled by a number of small firms. Look for addresses in the small advertisements in *Practical Parenting* or your local paper. The NCT (see Appendix) sell a comfortable range of lingerie and maternity swimwear.

USEFUL MATERNITY WEAR

◆ *For work, buy a good quality maternity skirt that will not lose its shape. Wear it with a variety of loose tops.*

◆ *For leisure wear, comfortable trousers can be worn with jersey tops and large T-shirts.*

◆ *Extra weight and swollen feet can ruin shoes. Buy one or two pairs to wear throughout pregnancy and discard them afterwards.*

◆ *If you intend to breastfeed buy loose, front-opening nightwear or use a big T-shirt. Your bust will be larger at the end of pregnancy and in the early weeks of breastfeeding.*

◆ *A serape, cape or poncho makes a comfortable outer garment in winter, or try to borrow a coat from a friend.*

◆ *For special occasions check your local paper and yellow pages for dress hire firms that include maternity wear. When choosing an outfit for a wedding, remember that the size and fit of your dress is more important than the style. A specialist bridal shop can offer you good advice.*

ANTENATAL CLASSES

Nothing can guarantee you an easy birth but if you go to antenatal classes you'll know what may happen and you'll be able to talk about pregnancy without feeling that your friends and family are stifling yawns! Classes vary in size, formality and the range of topics covered. You usually attend them later in pregnancy but good ones get booked up early.

NHS classes may be run by a midwife or shared between staff including health visitors and physiotherapists. They are free and can be excellent, although some hospitals give them low priority and a lot depends on the staff involved. A labour-ward tour may be included but you don't need to attend the classes to join it. NCT and other private classes usually go into more detail about birth. They are held at the teacher's home or a local hall for a charge, although this may be reduced in certain cases. Groups are small, the approach is informal and the teachers are usually knowledgeable and supportive.

Ask your midwife and your friends to recommend a class or check the notice board at the hospital or

‘ I was so ill for the first four months of pregnancy that I couldn't exercise and ended up feeling very sorry for myself. As soon as I was better I joined a pregnancy exercise class and met some super people on my wavelength.

We talk about anything, from how we're all secretly nervous about the birth to getting stranded in those incredible sex positions they show you in the books! I've learned that you don't have to be virtuous all the time. Sometimes we all meet up for a healthy swim and end up in a café eating cream buns instead! ’ GINA

YOUR PREGNANCY PLANNER – MONTHS 4-6

◆ *Attend monthly antenatal checkups. Write down questions to ask the midwife in case you forget.*

◆ *Improve your fitness – go for brisk walks, swim or join a pregnancy exercise class.*

◆ *Book antenatal classes now, and start to think about the sort of birth you hope to have (see page 84).*

◆ *Plan a holiday at home or abroad before you become too large to enjoy it, and before you face restrictions on air travel (see next page).*

◆ *Write to your employer at least 21 days before leaving work to retain your rights. Check qualifying dates for benefits (see page 46).*

◆ *Send for catalogues and check out baby equipment now – you may feel too tired to trek round the shops in late pregnancy.*

◆ *Make enquiries about alternative therapies (see page 73) for pregnancy discomforts and to help you feel good.*

---

clinic. The NCT and the Active Birth Centre (see Appendix) can give addresses of their trained teachers.

Here are some guidelines on choosing a class:

- A small, discussion-based class may suit you if you want to ask lots of questions and make your own decisions.
- If you are nervous about giving birth, ask friends to recommend a teacher who helps parents to feel relaxed and confident.
- Look for a large class where you can merge in, or arrange an individual class with an NCT or independent teacher if you prefer not to discuss birth with virtual strangers.
- Check the class is geared to fathers if your partner wants to be involved. Some classes treat men as onlookers, divide you into separate groups or only invite men to one or two sessions.
- Look for a women-only class if you are on your own.
- Ask whether alternative approaches will be covered if you want a natural birth. Some classes assume everyone will have drugs.
- It can be easier to share experiences with other parents and perhaps make lasting friendships in smaller groups.
- Ask whether classes tend to continue after the birth. You'll meet women who live nearby at classes run by your local midwife. On the other hand if you travel some distance to a class that friends have recommended you're likely to meet people who share your outlook on life.

QUESTIONS AND ANSWERS

Q: I am a lone parent and wish I had somebody to share my pregnancy and birth. I don't want to rely on my family, although they are very supportive. Where else could I get support?

A: Women often share the ups and downs of pregnancy and support each other, as some partners are not interested in the details of pregnancy or don't want to attend the birth. You may be able to develop a rewarding relationship with your midwife (see page 27), and you'll meet other women at antenatal classes. It may be easier to make friendships at exercise classes, or small birth preparation classes rather than at larger ones. The NCT (see Appendix) also organizes 'Bumps and Babes' sessions in some areas, where you can get to meet other mothers. If your family is supportive, letting them share your pregnancy can give pleasure to everyone. Organizations such as Gingerbread and the National Council for One Parent Families (see Appendix) can also give you practical and emotional support.

Q: We plan to go on holiday before our baby arrives. How can I make travelling easier, and how late in pregnancy can I fly with a scheduled airline?

A: Mid-pregnancy is a good time to go on holiday, and planning will make getting there and back less stressful. However you travel, wear loose, comfortable clothes and take plenty of snacks and mineral water.

In the car a cushion to place in the small of your back or to sit on may help. Your seat-belt should fit below your bump and across your chest, not under your arm. Sitting still for long periods makes you stiff, so allow extra time to stop every couple of hours and stretch your legs.

If you travel by plane, try to book a front or aisle seat so that you have more leg room and can walk about and visit the toilet more easily. Most airlines require a doctor's letter confirming you are fit to travel from 28 to 36 weeks, after which they will only carry you in an emergency. Individual airlines may vary, so check this. Remember to take your notes with you, just in case you need a doctor during your holiday!

Q: My brain cells are disappearing as fast as my waist expands! Why do I forget and lose things and what can I do about it?

A: Hormones cause some upheaval and part of your mind becomes taken up with the changes you are experiencing. Tiredness may also affect your ability to concentrate. The best solution is to accept it with good humour, rest more and use strategies to handle the overload. Start each day by listing things to do, putting a tick by the essentials and a query by the rest. Keep it on your pinboard or in your bag. A checklist by the door will remind you of vital things like closing windows or locking up. Tie your keys to your handbag with a long ribbon. Write reminders in your diary or on the back of your hand, or put tiny, coloured stickers where you will see them to jog your memory about appointments. If you streamline your life it will be much easier to cope.

6

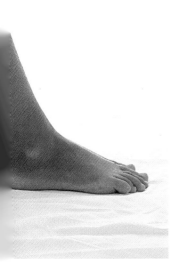

Plans and Choices

' You don't have to make choices. You can go along with what other people decide. But I love the challenge of learning about birth and I'd rather decide for myself what suits me. It's not so different from planning a special holiday. '

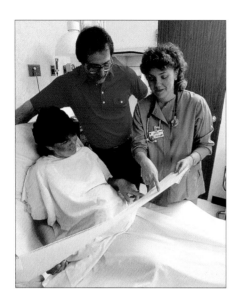

The midwife is explaining what the output from a fetal heart monitor means. You can share decisions about your treatment with her and your partner.

YOUR CHOICES FOR BIRTH

There are two, equally safe, basic approaches to care in labour. The first advocates intervention before a problem occurs in the hope of preventing it. The second favours watching carefully, but not intervening unless a problem actually arises. For example, if your labour was normal, but slow, a midwife who favoured the first approach might want to speed it up using a drip, in case you became too tired to push effectively. One who preferred the second approach might want to reassure you that everything was normal and help you to conserve energy for pushing.

If a complication occurs technology will be used to help, but if everything is normal there is no evidence that it makes birth safer. Intervention is a matter of judgement, which depends partly on the philosophy of the staff. Some feel that intervening prevents a difficult or dangerous situation arising. Others argue equally strongly that it can make further intervention necessary and actually cause problems that might not otherwise have arisen.

You may feel more confident giving birth using technology or you may feel that nature knows best.

Birth in hospital

The majority of births take place in hospital. In every labour a midwife will carry out routine checks such as listening to your baby's heartbeat and measuring your blood pressure. Beyond this hospitals have different approaches to labour. Some expect their staff to follow so many protocols that it considerably reduces your options; others are much more open to individual choices.

For a 'high-tech' birth you stay in bed throughout labour, with a hormone drip to control the contractions, a fetal monitor to record your baby's heartbeat and perhaps an epidural (see page 122) to numb sensation. One intervention sometimes leads to others, so read Chapter 10 to decide if this approach is right for you.

With a 'low-tech' approach there is no active intervention so long as you and your baby are fine. You don't have to stay in bed but could walk about, use a rocking chair, kneel on a mattress on the floor or lean over a bean bag to get comfortable. You could cope with contractions using relaxation and breathing techniques, but pain relief is always on hand if you need it.

'I decided not to give birth in my local hospital because it doesn't offer epidurals on request. I accept that there are some disadvantages to them but I don't see any point in suffering unnecessarily. If you wouldn't have a filling at the dentist without an injection, why give birth in pain?

I phoned a larger hospital twenty miles away to find out their approach, and then asked to be referred there. It's completely geared up to using technology and I feel secure knowing that everything will be monitored very closely. It also has excellent facilities in its special care baby unit, just in case.' MEGAN

Many hospitals have a mixed approach: basically low tech but with protocols regarding, for example, when a drip should be set up to speed up labour, or how long you could push before having an assisted delivery. These rules are often set by the consultant.

In most hospitals you can opt to stay for between six hours and a few days after your baby's birth. Even with a first baby some mothers go home within hours, and most leave within a day or two. Your midwife will visit you at home to check on your health and advise you on feeding and baby care.

The length of stay in hospital is an individual decision, depending on how you feel and whether it's your first baby or you have other children at home. If you plan an early discharge make sure you have help at home so that you can concentrate on your baby at first.

The staff at the hospital

Midwives' uniforms vary so the best way to find out who people are is to ask, or look at the name badges. Make a mental note of the colour of the belt, shape of the cap or whatever distinguishes the ranks at your hospital. If everything is normal you won't need a doctor's services, but there is always at least one on duty whom you could ask to see. Check the name badge, which will normally have a doctor's status on it. Here are some of the people you may see in hospital:

Midwifery sister: She may look after you during labour or postnatally. She also supervises the other midwives on the ward, so talk to her if you have a problem during your stay.

Staff midwife: She is qualified to care for you during pregnancy, normal

TO DECIDE WHICH APPROACH WILL SUIT YOU BEST

Tick the statements that you agree with:

◆ *I don't mind being wired to machinery in labour. (a)*

◆ *People who choose to have babies at home must be mad! (a)*

◆ *I prefer to move around and choose comfortable positions. (b)*

◆ *Labour is a natural event for most women. (b)*

◆ *I want my baby's heartbeat monitored by machine throughout the birth just in case anything goes wrong. (a)*

◆ *Relaxing in familiar surroundings should make labour easier. (b)*

◆ *Doctors and midwives usually know what's best for you. (a)*

◆ *I prefer no intervention as long as my baby is alright. (b)*

◆ *I want to avoid drugs if possible, as they have side effects. (b)*

◆ *Knock me out, please! I'd rather not feel a thing in labour. (a)*

The more 'a' statements you ticked the more likely that you'll feel reassured using birth technology. If you ticked mostly 'b' statements you may prefer a natural approach. Staff in large hospitals may be more geared to using technology than those in small hospitals or GP units. Home births are least likely to involve intervention in labour.

labour and delivery. After the birth she helps you to feed and care for your new baby.

Student midwife: A qualified nurse or direct entrant training to be a midwife. Depending on how far she has got she may observe your labour, perform examinations or deliver your baby. She will be under the supervision of a qualified midwife. You can refuse to have a student care for you although many women enjoy it as the midwives often explain everything in more detail when a student is around.

Other staff: Auxiliary nurses are unqualified but help with tasks such as serving meals. Nursery nurses are trained to look after babies in the nursery.

Obstetric physiotherapists have specialized in pregnancy and birth, and teach postnatal exercises or help with problems like backache.

Consultant obstetrician: A specialist in the medical problems of pregnancy and birth. He rarely attends a normal delivery but may be called in if there is a problem his registrar cannot deal with.

Senior registrar or Registrar: Specialists in obstetrics who usually deal with routine problems like a straightforward forceps delivery or Caesarean birth. The registrar is still training, although he often has considerable experience.

Senior house officer, or House officer: He or she has not specialized in obstetrics but might, for example, set up a drip if you need one. He is likely to be the first doctor called for any problem.

Student doctor: He or she is undergoing initial training so will be closely supervised. You can refuse care by a student if you wish.

Anaesthetist: You'll see him or her if you've decided to have an epidural or need a Caesarean birth.

Paediatrician: A specialist in baby problems, who will also check your baby to make sure that she's healthy before you leave hospital.

Breastfeeding counsellor: A mother who has breastfed her own children and who has trained to help other women. Not all hospitals have them.

Birth in a GP unit

GP units are run by local doctors and midwives. They can be separate institutions or attached to a hospital, and appeal to women who prefer a 'low-tech' approach. They are not, as is sometimes thought, reserved for women having second babies, women who live in certain areas, or for any other pre-determined reason.

If you have a domino delivery (see page 27) your midwife will bring you into the GP unit herself; otherwise you make your own way there when you are in labour. Your GP will be informed and may attend, although a community midwife usually supervises labour and delivers your baby. If a complication occurs you will be moved to a consultant unit in hospital.

Home birth

Home birth is as safe as hospital birth for most women, and it reduces risks such as infection and the negative effects of drugs and interventions. Even if you are over 35, small in stature, having your first baby or have a history of problems in pregnancy or labour you can still have a home birth. Some medical conditions, such as heart trouble, which could be stressed by labour, might make it unwise; but each case must be treated individually.

About a month before you are due your midwife will bring a sealed delivery pack of things she'll need at the birth, and discuss arrangements like having a clear space where she can put her supplies. When labour starts she'll assess you. If it's still early she may make other calls, but once labour is established she'll stay with you, contacting your GP if he wants to be there. She'll have pethidine, gas and oxygen and baby resuscitation equipment with her, although many women don't need them. She'll deliver your baby and stitch you if necessary. If a problem arises she'll transfer you to hospital. After the

'Some people prefer not to think about the birth in advance and just take things as they come, but I feel more confident if I've thought everything through.

I'm going to have my baby at my parents' house, where I usually stay while my husband is away. The midwife seems very happy about it, and my mother will look after my two year old daughter. When she was born my labour was quite short – only six hours – so if this labour is faster as second ones sometimes are I'd worry about getting to hospital. ' WENDY

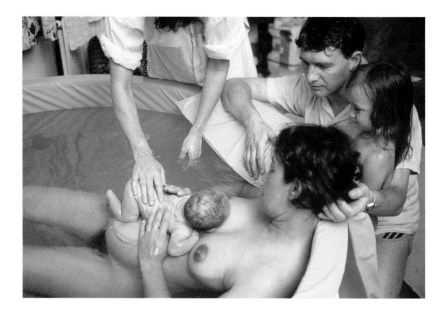

birth she'll visit frequently at first, then daily for about a week. You will be given a phone number to contact her for advice.

Home birth is usually a positive choice reflecting confidence in your ability to give birth, your midwife's skills and your family's support. You do need help – there's no holiday at home, no midwives to take over if you want a rest! Making everything ready before the birth takes effort and you'll need someone to keep the household running. To find out more about home birth, buy a book or contact AIMS (see Appendix).

' I knew nothing about water birth until I was 33 weeks pregnant, when a friend mentioned it. It sounded just right as I want as little intervention and as much privacy as possible during labour.

The midwives left us to find out about it for ourselves so I borrowed books from the library. My partner was supportive but he insisted that I have the baby in hospital.

I've hired an oval pool so that I can stretch out, or brace myself across it. When my contractions start we'll go to the hospital and my partner will put up the pool. It's been such fun planning the birth that I'm really looking forward to labour! ' RACHEL

Water birth

Labouring in water can help you feel relaxed and make it easier to cope with the pain. Some hospitals have a pool installed, or you can hire a birth pool. But water isn't the answer to every problem! It can help labour to progress but it cannot reduce dangerously high blood pressure, or deal with severe pain as effectively as an epidural. If a problem arises intervention may still be needed.

Water birth usually means using water to relieve pain and reduce the need for intervention during labour.

Left: Using a birth pool can be an effective way of relieving pain in labour.
Right: You may find it easier to relax in the familiar surroundings of your own home.

Some babies are born underwater because the birth is very fast, but most mothers leave the pool before delivery. It is thought to be very safe if guidelines about water temperature and things like the use of aromatherapy oils, how far dilated you must be before you enter the pool, and when you must leave it are followed.

Most practical difficulties can be overcome, although you may have to persevere to find someone supportive. Women have had water births with twins or a breech baby, when they normally use a wheelchair or after a previous Caesarean section. They have been arranged at a week's notice and have taken place in caravans and mobile homes. For more information, look for a book at your library or book shop, or ask your midwife or the Supervisor of Midwives at your hospital. If you want to talk to someone who has had a water birth, the NCT, AIMS (see Appendix) or one of the companies that hire birth pools (see small advertisements in *Practical Parenting*) may be able to put you in touch.

If you cannot arrange a water birth don't forget the bath! It may be too small to allow free movement but the water could still help to relieve pain.

Getting the birth you want

The easiest way to get the sort of birth that's right for you is to choose where to have your baby with care. Listen to your GP's advice, read Chapter 10 on help in labour and discuss all the possibilities. When you and your partner have weighed everything up, you're entitled to have your baby wherever you feel is right. Ask your GP or midwife to arrange it.

If you decide to have your baby in hospital canvass your midwife and friends who have recently had a baby for their views about different hospitals. One institution might be so accustomed to using birth technology that you'd find it hard if you wanted a natural birth, but another might not offer epidurals on request if you prefer this. You can phone a hospital antenatal clinic directly to find out what they offer. The staff should have time to discuss their approach straight away or to arrange for you to visit.

Think about asking some of the following questions.

For a high-tech birth:

- Can my baby be monitored electronically throughout my labour?
- Can I have an elective epidural even if I go into labour at night or during the weekend?
- How long would I be left before a drip was set up to increase the strength of my contractions?
- Would the technology be available even if the unit was busy?

For a low-tech birth:

- Provided the baby and I are both alright, how long can I go through labour without intervention?
- How will the staff help me to have a natural labour?
- What is the episiotomy rate here, and will the staff help me to deliver my baby without an episiotomy (see page 151) or tear?
- Can I use whatever position I like for the delivery?

CHOOSING NURSERY EQUIPMENT

Choosing baby clothes and decorating a nursery is fun, but don't buy everything before your baby arrives. You may receive gifts or change your mind in the light of experience. Here's a guide to the bare necessities you'll need for the early weeks:

Four vests: Wrap-over styles are easy to put on but the ties can be fiddly. Envelope necks fit well but pulling them over the baby's head takes a little practice. Bodysuits don't ride up but they may be outgrown more quickly.

Four stretchsuits/nightgowns: Stretchsuits are neat and easy to care for; nightgowns may make nappy changing easier at first.

Two cardigans/matinee jackets: Loose sleeves make dressing easy.

Two shawls: wrap your baby snugly in a cotton shawl or cot sheet to sleep at first. Draping a warm shawl over the car seat is easier than putting a snowsuit on your baby in the early weeks.

Snowsuit, hat, mittens (for a winter baby): A snowsuit with zips down both legs or right under the nappy and wide armholes makes dressing easier. Hats with ties stay on better.

Nappies: Disposable ones are more convenient. Buy small packs until you know what suits you then shop around to find the cheapest supplier and buy them in bulk. Re-usable terry squares or shaped nappies are environment friendly but need sanitizing powder. Terries need liners and pants, too. Some areas have a nappy washing service.

Changing equipment: You'll need a changing table or a changing mat to put on the floor, or on a table or chest of drawers at the right height. Cotton wool rolls are cheaper than balls. Buy small sizes of nappy cream until you find what suits you and your baby's skin.

Car safety seat: Birth to nine months seats with handles are easy to carry around. Two-way models (birth to four years) can be heavy and cumbersome in the early weeks. Some car seats do not fit in all cars, so check that the model you choose fits your vehicle.

Carrycot/Moses basket: A carrycot could be used as a pram; Moses baskets can be lighter and easier to carry around.

Pram/buggy: Choose from traditional or collapsible types and try pushing, folding and lifting different models. You could delay buying a pram or buggy by using a baby sling at first.

Four cot/pram sheets and two blankets: Look for easy-care labels. A shawl could double as a blanket, and vice versa.

Bath: A basin or washing up bowl will be fine at first. A simple plastic bath (with or without a stand) is heavy to lift with water in; one that rests on the big bath may be outgrown quickly.

Six bottles and sterilizing equipment (for bottlefeeding): Wide-necked bottles are easier to fill but may be more expensive. To sterilize them, cold water with sterilizing tablets or liquid is cheapest; electric steam sterilizers are convenient and use no chemicals; microwave sterilizers are compact.

Breast pads (for breastfeeding): Shaped pads are more expensive but may be more comfortable and stay in place better.

BREAST OR BOTTLEFEEDING?

Many parents believe, incorrectly, that formula milks are so sophisticated that there is little difference between them and breast milk. Breast milk contains hormones and enzymes that are not in formula milks because nobody knows what purpose they serve, plus substances to help fight bacterial and viral infections and combat childhood illnesses. It has all the right nutrients in the right amounts for your baby to grow healthily.

Breast milk adjusts to compensate if a baby is premature and alters as your baby grows and her needs change. It even dilutes in hot weather to satisfy a baby's thirst. There can be no doubt that breast is best for your baby.

Whether you breast or bottlefeed, the most important thing is a happy, rewarding feeding relationship with your baby. If you can't breastfeed or choose for various reasons to bottlefeed, there are compensations. It can be daunting to feel that your baby is completely dependent on you, and other people can take over when you bottlefeed. Babies often settle and sleep for longer because formula milk forms curds in the stomach so they feel more satisfied. If your baby is still hungry after a feed you can offer her more formula milk, whereas it takes a day or two of frequent feeding to increase your breast milk supply.

DISABLED PARENTING

Disabled parents' needs are as varied as their disabilities, but pregnancy can seem especially daunting if your GP or midwife has little practical experience of your particular disability.

The Disability Working Group of the Maternity Alliance (see Appendix) collates information on birth and disabilities. 'ParentAbility', an NCT group

(see Appendix), has a contact register linking parents with a wide range of disabilities, a pregnancy resource and information service, a database of practical information, and contacts for health professionals.

You may feel it's hard to plan ahead when you don't know the problems you are likely to face, but all parents discover how to handle pregnancy, birth and childcare by trial and error. Small children seem to adapt easily to a parent's disability, perhaps because disabled parents spend more time over each task and talk to their baby more, so that a co-operative relationship develops.

Looking after a baby is a challenge. Together you and your child will find ways to overcome your disability.

PREPARING A TODDLER

Parents who are delighted to be having another baby want their other child to feel the same. But small children have little idea of time so announcing the arrival of a baby six months ahead is like talking about Father Christmas in June! Usually, the younger the child the closer you can leave it to the birth before telling her.

Get your child used to the general idea of families first. Point out babies, read stories and talk about her friends' brothers and sisters so that she begins to understand what will happen.

Make changes in her life, such as starting playschool, well in advance. If she is moving to a new bedroom let her settle in before setting the cot up in her old room! In the last month she may enjoy helping to wash baby clothes or clean the pram. Get her used to a routine that will make life easier when you have less time after the baby arrives.

QUESTIONS AND ANSWERS

Q: I don't think I'll get the sort of birth I want at the hospital my GP has sent me to. My first baby is due in three weeks. Is it too late to have a home birth?

A: You're entitled to change your mind and be referred to a different hospital or a GP unit, or to choose a home birth at any time. Talk to your GP. If he or she feels home birth is risky in your case listen to the reasons. Making a decision means taking responsibility for the outcome so be sure in your own mind about what you want.

However, don't be put off by initial opposition. No one wants battles, especially when pregnant, but opposition often melts away when you show you've thought something through and are determined. You don't need your GP's agreement to have a home birth. If your own midwife is unsympathetic and you don't know another one to approach direct, write to the Supervisor of Community Midwives at your local hospital keeping copies of your letters. She must ensure you're provided with a midwife who'll give you total care and any necessary back-up.

The NCT booklet 'Giving Birth at Home' has useful information and a sample letter. Your Regional Health Information Service or AIMS (see Appendix) will help if you have any difficulties.

Q: What should I look for when choosing a nursing bra?

A: It's best to delay buying nursing bras until your baby's head has engaged (see page 52). When the head is high your ribs expand to allow more space, so a bra that fits well may be loose around the ribcage after the birth.

A nursing bra should be comfortable and substantial enough to play an effective supporting role. Look for a broad band to give support under the cups. The bra should fit without gaping, but with space to slip your hand between the top of the cup and your breast, to give room for expansion after the birth. Stretch straps are too bouncy when breastfeeding and elastic loses shape with repeated washing. Cotton rich fabric allows your skin to breathe. Zips or front openings are a matter of taste, but avoid seams that press and mark your skin as this could lead to pressure problems during breastfeeding.

Q: How much equipment do new babies really need? We are not well off and I'm worried about overspending our budget.

A: Not as much as many people imagine, and there are ways to economize. Look through catalogues and collect information, but delay spending until you really need something. You may find you can borrow equipment from friends or relatives, or improvise after your baby arrives.

Most large towns have shops that sell nearly-new clothes and equipment but do look up *Which* reports on safety standards before you buy. Economy is often a necessity, but if your heart really longs for something rather extravagant, consider the lift it could give you in return for economizing sensibly the rest of the time. Treat yourself if possible. Babies are fun as well!

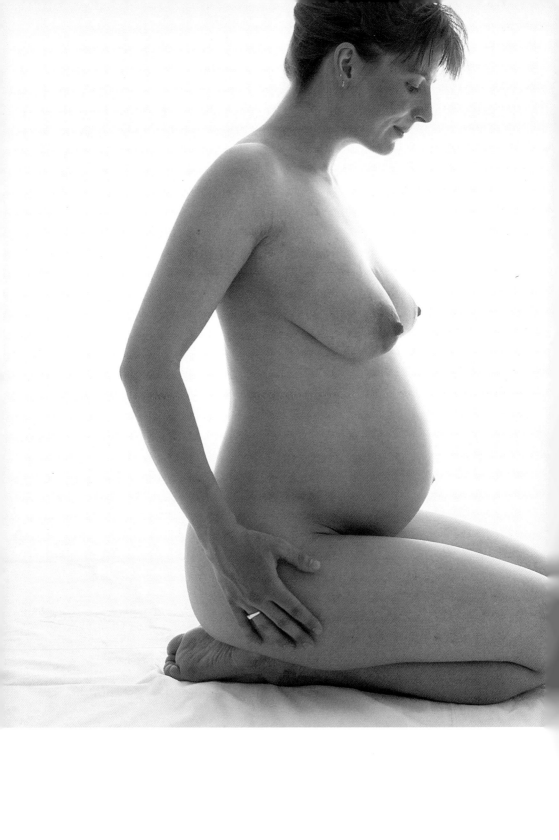

7

Late Pregnancy

(MONTHS 7–9)

' *The last few weeks, and the finish is almost in sight. I feel a mixture of terror, excitement, boredom and elation. The days drag, yet I want to hang on and savour every last bit of them. Once they are over life will never be the same again.* '

Seventh month: This baby is already lying head down, but about 25 per cent of babies will be breech at this stage.

Eighth month: Compare this picture with the one on page 36 to see how much space your baby takes up, moving internal organs to make room.

Ninth month: Your baby stores fat under his skin in the last month so he looks much rounder and plumper.

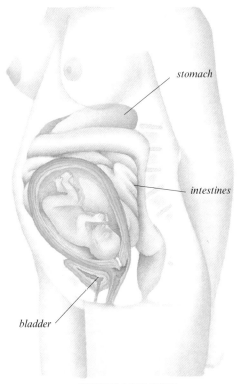

SEVEN MONTHS

HOW YOUR BABY DEVELOPS

In the last three months of pregnancy your baby's breathing and swallowing rhythms become increasingly well regulated. Cartilage develops to give shape to his ears, his eyelids open, his fingernails grow and the soft dark body hair (lanugo) disappears. Fat stores build up to provide energy and regulate his temperature.

Your baby receives antibodies to common bugs and childhood illnesses such as chickenpox through the placenta, which also produces gamma globulin to help both of you to fight infection. Up to 1¾ pints (1 litre) of constantly renewed amniotic fluid filters out waste products from the uterus and his skin is protected with creamy vernix to stop it getting waterlogged.

At 28 weeks the average baby measures about 14in (35cm) and weighs 2lb (nearly 1kg). Each week for the next month he grows roughly ½in (1cm) and puts on ½lb (225g), although this growth pattern gradually diminishes and almost stops a week or so before birth. Hormone levels in the placenta

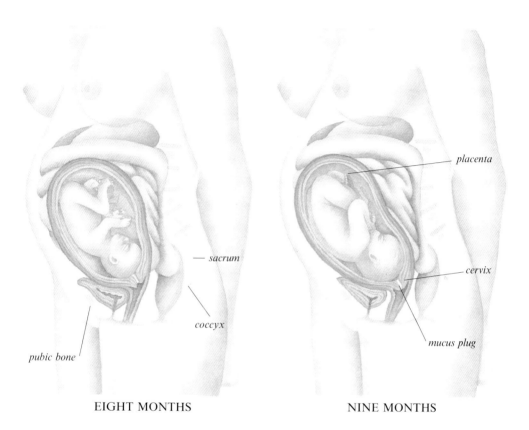

sacrum

coccyx

pubic bone

placenta

cervix

mucus plug

EIGHT MONTHS

NINE MONTHS

change, the uterus is fully stretched and the baby has little room to move. It's time to start the short journey into a new and independent life!

The majority of babies born after 32 weeks survive nowadays, and delivery after 37 weeks is considered normal. By this time the baby's lungs have matured and surfactant, a soap-like substance in the amniotic fluid, makes breathing easier by preventing the lung surfaces from sticking together. After 40 weeks a baby is well equipped to enter the world, although he will still need loving care for months and years ahead.

HOW YOU MAY FEEL

Most women slow down a little, but if you are fit and experience no complications, late pregnancy can be very enjoyable. You may feel at your happiest and most relaxed. A large bump usually elicits well-intentioned support and kindliness from other people, not to mention relieving you of unwelcome social obligations!

' *My pregnancy has changed our lives in little ways. I haven't stopped doing anything, but I've pulled over from the fast lane and I amble along in the slow lane. My husband has given up his share of the duvet and sleeps right on the edge of the bed because I've taken over the rest.*

He has to keep a sense of humour and think for both of us. Last week the ceiling of a room we were decorating needed painting and he was going out. I asked him to get the stepladder for me before he went. He refused, and came home with a ball of wool and a pair of knitting needles! With three weeks to go I reluctantly took the hint. ' KAREN

Many women have mixed feelings about giving up work; some count the days until they leave, while others dread the loss of income, stimulus and companionship. Every change in life has its good and bad aspects. You will be able to rest more, but you may find that time passes slowly without the rhythm of work and you may become bored with your pregnancy. The last few weeks can seem to stretch ahead interminably if you are already uncomfortable and heavy. See the next page and page 70 for suggestions on how to stay well.

You may feel increasingly worried about your baby's health and feel vulnerable to casual, throwaway comments, especially from health professionals. You may be panicky about birth and motherhood as they draw inescapably nearer, or you may swing wildly from depression to euphoria. By the ninth month this is usually overtaken by a positive longing to see your baby and to have your body to yourself again.

To create and give birth to a new human being is very special, but the last few weeks can be uncomfortable. As your baby grows your uterus takes up space under your lungs which can leave you short of breath. When your baby's head engages (see page 52) you'll breathe more easily, but will probably need to go to the toilet more often! Your uterus may cause pain under your ribs, or an itchy or tight, stretched feeling in the skin over your bump. Some women feel a sharp pain when the baby butts their bladder.

By now, most babies have definite waking periods with stronger kicks and movements. Some seem less active while others knock a book off your lap or wake you up at night. You may have difficulty sleeping because your pelvis aches. The hormones that soften your ligaments to make the birth easier may also contribute to cramp, varicose veins, piles and heartburn (see pages 72-3).

Your breasts will enlarge and they may leak colostrum, a creamy fluid present in your breasts before milk is produced. Some women experience nasal congestion, nose or gum bleeds, thrush or a copious but inoffensive vaginal discharge. Others find their ankles start to swell (see page 102) or they suffer from carpal tunnel syndrome, where fluid compresses the nerves in the wrist causing tingling or numbness. Your GP may suggest an orthopaedic wrist support and the NCT (see Appendix) have a helpful leaflet about this problem. These symptoms of late pregnancy can be tiresome, but do see your doctor if they seem excessive.

You may feel your tummy become firm for about 30 seconds as Braxton Hicks contractions tone up your uterus. These practice contractions may be barely noticeable, or so strong (especially if it is not your first baby) that you have to stop and breathe gently over them as though you were in labour. If you're fed up with your appearance a new hairstyle or a good cut could give your morale a boost, and save time later on.

RELATIONSHIP WITH YOUR PARTNER

Your relationship with your partner will change during pregnancy, especially if this is your first baby. Discuss the future, so that you can find common ground that allows each of you to get something of what you want from your partnership. When a baby arrives a cosy twosome does not change magically into a cosy threesome! You will both be concerned about your baby's welfare but will also have individual needs to be fulfilled by negotiation.

It's normal and healthy for a woman to focus on her changing body and the birth, but not to the exclusion of all else. If you are too self-absorbed it can be tedious for your partner. He will support you in many little ways, so try to respond to his needs too. If he attends classes or listens to 'baby talk' for your sake, show equal interest in something that primarily concerns him.

When you are adding to your family, or your partner has children from a previous relationship, he may show less interest in your pregnancy. This can be disappointing if it's your first baby, so tell him how you feel. Some men need reminding to give extra help in late pregnancy, although many fathers willingly take on responsibility for other children. On the other hand, if this is your partner's first baby, give him the chance to enjoy being a first-time father by going to antenatal classes with him, even if you don't feel the need.

Taking pleasure in your partner's company helps to fan the flames of love. Try to find activities that you both enjoy, can do together and can keep up after your baby arrives. Family life is challenging; pregnancy is an opportunity to deepen your understanding of each other's needs and strengthen the bond between you.

STAYING WELL

The extra weight, softening hormones and gymnastic ability of your baby can make late pregnancy uncomfortable. You will feel better if you use your body well and conserve energy. Maintaining good posture (see page 44) prevents unnecessary muscle tension and painful strains to softened ligaments.

It can be frustrating to tire quickly, especially if you have work to do, but you'll help yourself if you listen to your body and rest before you become over-tired. Fifteen minutes of complete relaxation is worth an hour of half-resting with your mind whizzing around things you feel you should be doing instead!

COPING WITH LATE PREGNANCY

◆ *Never stand when you could sit down, or sit when you could lie down. Make sure you stand, sit or lie without twisting your body.*

◆ *A v-shaped pillow can provide some comfortable support when you are sitting in a chair or propped up in bed.*

◆ *To relax completely for five minutes, sit comfortably with your shoulders down and hands palm uppermost in your lap. Concentrate on the sensation in one hand and imagine it gradually growing warmer.*

◆ *For a quick pick-me-up, mash a banana and blend it with a glass of milk, a little honey and two tablespoons of natural yoghurt.*

◆ *Try to make some friends locally, to stand you in good stead after your baby is born. Exercise and antenatal classes are good places to meet other pregnant women.*

◆ *If your pregnancy seems endless and you feel low, lift your spirits with an outing, or treat yourself to a massage or a special luxury to keep up your morale.*

Relaxing and sleeping

Most women sleep less soundly at the end of pregnancy. You might be woken by night sweats, but more often it is the baby's movements and the call of nature! Have a glass of water beside the bed as your body needs extra fluid during pregnancy and dehydration can cause slight headaches.

If you and your partner sleep badly because you are restless, perhaps he could take to the spare bed occasionally to get an unbroken night. A packet of biscuits, a thermos of cocoa or a good book, within reach, may help if you can't get back to sleep once you have woken. On the positive side, at least insomnia gets your body prepared for night feeds after your baby arrives!

When you are really exhausted you will sleep soundly in any position, but if you are having difficulty relaxing or sleeping you may find some of the positions illustrated opposite comfortable.

ANTENATAL CHECKS

From 28 weeks you'll probably have antenatal checks every fortnight and in the last month they'll be weekly. If you see the same staff each time you can build a relationship with the midwife or members of her team, so that you feel able to ask questions, seek advice or discuss any worries you might have.

The checks will be familiar by now, but the midwife will also determine your baby's position (although this can change), make sure that he is growing well and look out for potential problems such as swelling or pre-eclampsia (see page 102).

Relaxing and Sleeping *Try lying on your side with a pillow between your knees to reduce the strain on your ligaments. You may like to put another pillow under your bump*

Prop yourself up using a bean bag or two pillows under your knees to take the strain off your lower back. This position can help you to avoid heartburn.

Sit in a chair with a v-shaped pillow supporting your head. You could put another pillow on a small stool to support your legs.

KICK CHART							Name: Sue						
Week: 34							Week: 35						
Day:	M	T	W	Th	Fr	Sa	Su	M	T	W	Th	Fr	Sa	Su
Time													
9.00													
9.30													
10.00													
10.30													
11.00													
11.30													
12.00													
12.30													
1.00													
1.30													

'Count to 10' kickchart: You start counting at the same time each day and mark the time of the tenth kick on your chart. A baby who is kicking happily as usual is thriving.

A kickchart is sometimes given towards the end of pregnancy to check that the placenta is working well. The midwife will explain what to do, but tell her if it worries instead of reassuring you.

You record your baby's kicks over a given period and after a few days a pattern emerges so that you know what is 'normal' for you. If you don't feel your baby move one day, or there's any marked change such as less frequent kicks, tell your midwife. Don't leave it until the next day!

Swelling

At least three-quarters of women suffer from fluid retention at some time in pregnancy. Your legs or ankles may swell in hot weather or at the end of the day. You may wake up to find your fingers tingling or your rings feel tight. If you cannot get your shoes on or your hands or face become puffy, contact your midwife or GP.

Don't restrict your intake of liquids or salt unless you are told to. Wear support tights and sit with your feet up whenever possible. If your fingers swell, wriggle them to help ease discomfort; gently wind string around your finger from the tip so that a ring will slip off when you unwind it.

Mild swelling can result from the normal fluid increase of pregnancy. If a hollow remains when you press the skin for 30 seconds and let go, you have oedema. This is not dangerous in itself, but it can be a symptom of pre-eclampsia which needs medical attention, so consult your GP.

Pre-eclampsia

This illness affects both the mother and baby and is cured by the delivery of the baby and placenta. Early in a normal pregnancy your arteries adapt to accommodate an increasing blood supply so that your baby gets more food and oxygen as he grows. For an unknown reason, possibly genetic plus an environmental trigger, in about one in 10 pregnancies the blood vessels fail to adapt. The placenta gets insufficient blood, the baby doesn't grow well, the mother's blood pressure rises and she may suffer symptoms such as oedema and impaired kidney function.

In most cases pre-eclampsia does no lasting harm. Worry and stress do not cause it; rest and relaxation do not cure it. In very mild cases, extra rest may help and your blood pressure might be checked daily at home.

However, for one in a 100 first pregnancies and fewer subsequent ones, the illness is serious enough to lead to convulsions or even coma unless it is treated. You will be monitored in hospital so that symptoms such as high blood pressure can be treated with drugs. Depending on the severity of the illness you may go into labour spontaneously and have a normal delivery, or you might be induced or delivered by Caesarean section.

Pre-eclampsia is usually suspected if you have at least two out of three classic symptoms: raised blood pressure, oedema and protein in your urine. Repeated scans may show your baby is not growing well, or abnormalities may show up in a blood test. In rare cases where the illness comes on suddenly there may be pain in the upper abdomen, vomiting, visual disturbances or a very severe headache. Contact your GP about such symptoms, although they don't necessarily mean you have pre-eclampsia.

Poor growth

A baby may fail to grow properly if his mother is ill, smokes or has an unhealthy lifestyle, or if the placenta fails to supply all his needs. The placenta reaches maturity somewhere between 32 and 34 weeks and then gradually becomes less efficient, although most will sustain all a baby's needs for more than 42 weeks.

If a baby seems smaller than expected for the stage of pregnancy you have reached, intra-uterine growth retardation (IUGR) would be suspected. Ultrasound scans (see page 56), repeated at intervals, could confirm or refute the diagnosis.

Poor growth is more common in first pregnancies, and fifth or later ones. Many individual factors probably contribute to it, but it is unlikely to happen if your weight is normal, you are well nourished, and you don't smoke. If you attend regular antenatal checks any problem associated with poor growth, such as anaemia or kidney disease, can be treated early.

If poor growth is diagnosed you may go into hospital for bed rest or medication to improve placental blood flow. In extreme cases your baby would be delivered early. Although prevention and treatment of poor growth are preferable, even when they are unsuccessful such babies often eventually catch up.

‘ *To be perfectly honest, I'm fed up with pregnancy. I can't sleep properly or eat a decent meal or walk more than a few yards before sitting down to rest. My ankles swell each evening and I haven't felt like going out for weeks.*

I know it's well-intentioned, but I've found it hard to adjust to being 'public property'. Sometimes people I hardly know come up and pat my bump and it's hard not to resent it. Pregnancy is not my favourite time of life. I can't wait for the baby to arrive. ’ SIOBHAN

YOUR BABY'S POSITION

Somewhere between 34 and 40 weeks most babies turn head down and settle deeply in the pelvis. But babies are individuals: some wait for extra softening hormones produced at the beginning of labour before they engage and others just stay bottom down. Once a baby is head down and fully engaged he rarely changes position.

If you feel a firm area down one side of your tummy it may be your baby's back. Ask your midwife if your baby is lying in an anterior position. This is a good lie: with his back to your tummy he can tuck his chin on his chest, fit neatly into your pelvis and turn slightly to emerge at the birth.

If he lies with his back towards to your back (posterior), his chin may not tuck in so well and he has further to rotate to pass under your pubic arch, which could make the birth longer. Try kneeling on all fours as often as possible so that gravity helps his spine, which is heaviest, to move round. It sometimes helps to gyrate your hips whichever way feels most comfortable, to encourage him to rotate.

A baby who lies bottom down and refuses to budge by the recommended turn-by date may simply be a late starter. Sit up straight to give your baby more room. Keep a bottle of baby lotion in the fridge to soothe the sore patch where his head lies. Try the remedies for heartburn (see page 73) if this is proving a problem.

If your baby does not turn head down spontaneously by 34 weeks you could encourage him using the methods described on page 106. Your doctor might also try, especially if it is not your first baby. You will be asked to lie on your back with your knees up and relax while the doctor massages your tummy, helping your baby to slip round. This is called external version; no force is used and the attempt will stop if your baby clearly does not want to move.

Being pregnant again is great! I haven't had time to worry about every little thing and I've enjoyed sharing it with Emily, my two year old, who loves babies. She's very knowing so we had to tell her quite early because everyone else knew, but she has no idea of time and I'm sure she thinks we're making it all up! Now I'm almost there I can't wait to see her face when she finds out we're not.

We bought bunk beds for her bedroom and left her cot up. The first night she slept in it. Then she decided she was a big girl and wanted to sleep in the bed, so we went to buy a duvet and she chose the cover. Now she happily tells people the cot is for her baby. ZOE

After 36 weeks it's sensible to discuss breech birth (see page 160) with the midwife in case your baby doesn't turn. Only three per cent of babies remain in a breech position at birth.

Your baby's position has quite a lot to do with how your labour goes. If he lies well curled up and with his spine to one side of your tummy, your labour may be easier. But remember that being well prepared can also make your labour easier. Learning to relax and being realistic about labour (see page 132) will help you to cope if your baby adopts a less favourable position.

PRESENTATIONS FOR BIRTH

Above: Right occipito posterior (ROP) where the baby faces the mother's abdominal wall.

Below: Frank breech where the thighs are flexed but the legs are pointed upwards. The arms are around the legs.

Above: Left occipito anterior (LOA) is the most common presentation. The baby faces the mother's spine.

Below: Footling breech where the thighs are only slightly flexed and baby's foot is born first.

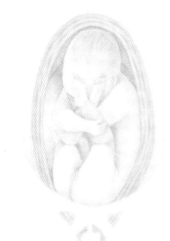

Above: Full breech presentation where the thighs are flexed against the body and the knees are bent.

◆ *Antenatal checks are once a fortnight; weekly for the last month.*

◆ *Find out if your employer needs a letter from your GP if you want to continue working after you become eligible for maternity leave.*

◆ *Go to an experienced fitter for nursing bras (see page 93).*

◆ *Hire maternity wear for any special occasions. Look in your local paper or Yellow Pages for advertisements.*

◆ *Pack your suitcase (see page 116) about six weeks before your due date. Buy or hire a car seat (see page 91) to bring your baby home in.*

◆ *If you have a toddler, make arrangements (with back-up) for his care while you are in labour. Buy a small present for him, ready for his first meeting with his sister or brother.*

◆ *Write your birthplan (see page 118). There's still time to alter your booking if you want to have your baby somewhere else.*

◆ *Arrange to hire a TENS machine (see page 122) if your hospital or midwife cannot lend you one. Hire a radiopager to ensure you can contact your partner when you go into labour. Look in Yellow Pages or the small advertisements in* Practical Parenting.

◆ *Arrange outings for after your 'date' as you might go overdue!*

◆ *Record a message on your answering machine if you need a rest from too many phone calls before and after the birth.*

QUESTIONS AND ANSWERS

Q: I am 35 weeks pregnant and my baby is lying in a breech position. Should I ask my doctor to turn him, or can I do anything myself to encourage this?

A: Your doctor would only decide to intervene after considering your history – for example, whether you have had other children, how firm your muscles are and the position of your placenta. You could certainly try to encourage your baby to turn using positions or alternative therapies, although babies are individuals and some prefer being bottom down.

Put a bean bag or a pile of pillows on the floor and make a hollow in them for your bump. Lie on your front with your bottom higher than your hips for about 20 minutes. Relax and try to 'will' your baby round. After a while (not always at the first attempt) your baby may float free of your pelvis and do a somersault. Get up slowly (you may feel rather shaken) and walk around or squat to help fix your baby's head in your pelvis. Alternatively you could lie back with your hips raised on pillows and your knees bent and roll gently from side to side for 10 minutes three times a day. Stop if you feel light-headed or uncomfortable.

An acupuncturist might suggest applying pressure, acupuncture needles or heat from a singed herb (moxibustion) to a point on the outer edge of the little toe to help your baby to turn. A homeopath might recommend a single dose of Pulsatilla at high potency. If you want to try alternative therapies (see page 73), do consult a qualified practitioner.

Q: Last week a van driver failed to give way to me on a roundabout and almost hit the side of my car. I was unhurt but very shaken and later that day my baby kicked wildly for two hours. Could the accident have harmed him, and should I stop driving?

A: There's no reason to stop driving short distances right up to delivery day, provided you feel fine, fit behind the steering wheel and can comfortably fasten your seat belt. You should not drive yourself to hospital when you are in labour, and you may find long journeys tiring in late pregnancy whether you are the driver or a passenger (see page 81).

A baby may react with a period of greater than normal activity after any sudden shock, such as an accident or receiving bad news. Rest for a few hours to give your body a chance to recover, and if you are worried for any reason contact your GP or midwife.

Q: I'm 34 weeks pregnant and my midwife says that my baby's head has engaged. I thought this happened at 36 weeks, so does it mean that my baby will be born early?

A: It suggests that your baby is lying in a favourable position and your pelvis is roomy. First babies engage on average at 36 weeks, but later babies may not do so until you're in labour. Once your baby has engaged he has resolved the question of whether your pelvis is big enough for this. Every baby has to engage at some stage in order to be born normally, but it doesn't predict when you will go into labour. The timing depends on the size of your pelvis, how firm your abdominal muscles are, the amount of hormones flowing and your baby's position.

Q: My teenage daughters from my husband's first marriage want to be present at the birth. We have asked my mother-in-law to look after our three year old son, who adores his Gran. How can I prepare my step-daughters for the birth and make sure that my son does not feel left out?

A: Your daughters might like to look at books or a video with you, and they should be aware of the realities of birth. Tell them they can leave at any time if they wish, and explain circumstances when they might not be able to be there. Make sure that your midwife is happy for them to be present, so that they will feel welcome.

If a day spent with Gran's undivided attention is a treat for your son, he is unlikely to feel left out. He will not be at the birth but he can still be part of the celebration. Suggest that your mother-in-law might like to help him draw on balloons with thick felt tips and decorate a card for the baby. Pack a small surprise in his suitcase for him to find – and don't forget one for Gran, too!

8

Preparing for the Birth

' There's so much to think about when a baby is born. It's not just learning to relax and help yourself to handle the birth; it's all the practical little details like remembering to pay the milkman and feed the cat! '

WHAT MAKES LABOUR EASIER?

Labour is easier if you have space to relax, and privacy so that you can let go of your inhibitions and flow with the rhythm of the contractions. Intrusions, or distractions such as moving from one place to another, may disturb this rhythm. Darkness or subdued lighting can help you to use instinct rather than rational thought. You need to feel safe and at ease in the place where you give birth, and with the people who care for you. Otherwise, the delicate mechanisms of the natural birth process may be upset.

Preparing for the birth will help to make your labour easier by giving you confidence in your body and trust in your instincts so that you cope in the way that feels right to you at the time.

TOUR OF THE LABOUR SUITE

Most hospitals provide tours of the labour suite, often at evenings or weekends so that partners can attend. Phone the hospital to check details, or ask at your next antenatal visit. Here are some things you could find out:

- What facilities are available? Is there a mattress for the floor, a bean bag, rocking chair or large bath? What are the arrangements for refreshment and what are the car parking regulations?
- What use could you make of the furniture in the room you'll be in during labour? A cupboard might be the right height to lean on; moving the bed might give you more space, for example.
- How do the staff feel about monitoring (see page 148), episiotomies (see page 151) or delivery positions (see pages 114-15)? Are there hospital policies regulating them, and can these be varied?
- Where should you go at night? Hospital security procedures may mean the door you normally use is locked.

RELAXATION AND BREATHING FOR LABOUR

Labour is a physical task, like running a marathon. If you run stiffly the race is harder. When your uterus contracts strongly other muscles tend to join in, but if you relax it works more effectively and your body's natural pain killing hormones flow. During labour you'll need to keep checking so that you can release tension before it engulfs you. Pull your shoulders down and let them go, part your lips to loosen your jaw, turn your hands palm upwards.

'I ignored the birth at first. Now I've started to face up to it and it seems like a huge wall. I'm like a yo-yo, one minute whining that I'll never cope and the next minute feeling that labour's no problem and it'll be all right on the night! I'm going to antenatal classes and on a tour of the labour suite. Once I've got labour in proportion I know I'll be fine. **'** SARA

110

Relaxation and breathing are intertwined – if you relax deeply your breathing will adjust to the best level for you. Some women prefer to concentrate on breathing control to help them relax and give them something to think about. Use slow, gentle breathing, pausing slightly between breaths and letting your breathing rise to your middle or upper chest during the contractions if it's more comfortable. Your body will tell you what feels best. Always concentrate on the 'out' breath to avoid hyperventilation, but if you do start to feel light-headed, cup your hands over your face and breathe into them slowly until the sensation passes.

Breathing for labour

Ask your partner to help you practise breathing for labour until you feel confident using different areas of your chest.

Right: Full chest: Relax consciously and aim your breathing towards the warmth of your partner's hands, so that he feels a slight movement below your waist. During labour use full chest breathing unless your contractions make mid or upper chest breathing easier.
Below: Mid chest: Breathe so that your bra gets tighter and your partner feels the movement with this hands.
Below right: Upper chest: Breathe lightly with little huffs, using the top part of your chest.

POSITIONS FOR LABOUR

The mechanics of giving birth suggest that some positions will work better than others in certain circumstances.

As your uterus contracts it rises up and forwards, so leaning in this direction lets the contractions work with gravity. Lying back makes them work against it. If you're upright your baby's head presses against your cervix, speeding up dilation. Positions where your thighs are flexed and wide apart will stretch the ligaments that join the three bones of your pelvis, thereby giving your baby extra room.

When your body is horizontal, gravity takes your baby away from your cervix and towards your spine, abdomen or side, depending on your position.

Sit reversed on a chair padded with a pillow. Relax onto another pillow placed on the chair back.

Stand, leaning onto your partner, the wall or a piece of furniture during contractions.

Sit with your knees apart, leaning onto your partner.

Some women find their contractions are more effective when they lie down because they are able to relax better; others find that lying down eases the pain of a very fast labour.

Adopting positions that use gravity and open your pelvis, such as the ones illustrated below, often makes labour easier. You could use pillows to reduce pressure on your knees or thighs. The positions suggested for relaxation on page 101 may also be comfortable.

There are no hard and fast rules – women are different and what works for one may not help another. Don't feel that you ought to use certain positions because they're supposed to be best. Just experiment to find those in which you can relax well.

Sit on the padded rim of a bucket. Plant your feet squarely so that you can rock or move your body freely.

Spread your knees to make space for your bump and lean forwards onto your hands.

Kneel on something soft and lean onto your partner's lap or the bed.

Stand to deliver while your partner holds you under the arms. He could lean against a wall and bend his knees to protect his back.

Stand or semi-squat, supported by your partner and a midwife. They should bend their knees as they take your weight.

POSITIONS FOR DELIVERY

Many women deliver on their backs because no one suggests anything else. This isn't ideal because your baby moves against gravity and puts extra pressure on the perineum (the delicate tissue around the birth canal) as it thins out. To move from your back to your knees, ask your partner to stand beside the bed to help you. Slide the outer border of one foot towards your bottom. Push on the bed with your arm to raise your body. Roll over to kneel facing the side of the bed, with your arms around your partner's neck. The midwife will help you deliver from behind.

Pushing is easier in upright positions because gravity helps and your tail bone swings back, giving your baby more room to move. If the birth is rapid you could move onto your side. Women who stand to give birth often report less damage to the perineum. It's up to you to choose your position. You will not know what's right until the time, but try out these positions in advance.

Lie on your side with your knees
bent. Your partner supports your
upper leg during contractions.

Kneel on the bed leaning onto the
headboard, pillows or a bean bag.
This position helps to prevent a tear.

Squat and lean into your
partner's lap with your
feet flat and your arms
over his knees.

YOUR LABOUR BAG

Your hospital will provide a list of things to bring in, but here are some practical suggestions from mothers for what to take:

◆ *Light clothing, as hospitals are very warm.*

◆ *Travel or paper fan or mineral water spray to keep cool.*

◆ *Crushed ice in a thermos flask (to suck); cool box with mineral water or fruit juice.*

◆ *Flannel or natural sponge to moisten lips; lip salve.*

◆ *Squashy ice pack, pack of frozen peas or wooden back massager to ease backache; oil or talc for massage.*

◆ *Cassette recorder, music or story tapes, headphones; jigsaw, games, books to pass the time.*

◆ *Treats to keep your spirits up; snacks for your partner; peppermint teabags for wind (especially after a Caesarean).*

◆ *Cushion, bean bag, small stool or bucket to sit on.*

◆ *Socks for cold feet.*

◆ *Poster or calendar to focus on; camera; money for the phone.*

YOUR PARTNER'S FEELINGS ABOUT LABOUR

Most men are excited at the thought of being present at the birth, but they may be worried about not knowing what to do, or perhaps fainting at the sight of blood. Films and videos often give a false impression of labour because, like TV holiday programmes where the sun always shines, they are selective in what they present. The birth of your own baby is usually less dramatic but much more emotional and exciting. If your partner is anxious it will help if he attends antenatal classes with you.

YOUR BIRTH PARTNER

Your birth partner could be anyone close to you, although it's usually your baby's father. Midwives have more than one woman to look after, so his role is to make your labour easier by offering comfort, encouragement and loving concern. Even if your birth partner does nothing except stay close to you, you'll value his (or her) presence. However, sensitive support, freely given at the right moment, is an added bonus since it raises your pain threshold and makes it easier for you to cope.

' *I've never been afraid of giving birth. I'm more worried about losing control and not being able to make my own decisions. Right from the beginning I read everything I could about birth. I've learned to be more flexible because now I understand why things happen that can't be avoided.* ' ANNE-MARIE

116

Here are some suggestions for birth partners:

- Take care of her physical needs. Help her change position, keep her cool, put crushed ice in the water she sips, change the music tapes and generally give her your attention. Never appear to be bored, or more interested in the newspaper or the labour machinery than in her!

- Keep her morale up if labour is long and her energy flags. Think of labour as a series of short intervals, not one long stretch of time. In the early stages, you could read funny anecdotes or poetry to her, play 'I Spy', choose your baby's name, walk round the corridors with her, or produce an unexpected treat.

- Create a positive atmosphere, however her labour goes. She cannot relax if you are tense, so assume an air of calm like a swan gliding on the surface while paddling fast underneath!

- Help her to relax. Watch for tight face muscles or clenched teeth. Keep reminding her to relax her shoulders. Some women can't bear to be touched during labour; others like their shoulders massaged or their hair stroked. When the contractions are strong, redouble your efforts to keep her relaxed.

- Help her to focus on something other than the contractions. Describe a place you both know so that she can imagine it; stroke her palm, or name groups of muscles so that she can relax them one by one. Most women find idle chatter distracting but counting can be helpful: look into her eyes and count slowly aloud from the beginning of the contraction until it's over.

- Act as a physical support. Put your arms around her so that she can lean on you, if necessary, during contractions. Let her drape herself over you when she's kneeling, or sit on the floor using you as a sort of armchair. If she asks for support when she's pushing protect your back by bending your knees.

- Act as her spokesman. Interpret her wishes to the staff, and vice versa. She'll rely on you when the contractions are strong and may appear not to hear anyone else. Be sensitive to her wishes. She may genuinely change her mind about some things, like accepting pain relief.

- Remind her to breathe gently, emphasizing the 'out' breath. Tension causes changes in breathing rhythm and rate, so concentrating on quiet breathing will help her relax.

- Massage her back, mop her brow, praise her efforts. Encouragement is more helpful than sympathy when a woman is trying hard to cope without any drugs. Stay supportive even if she gets cross with you – she really wants you there! After the birth reassure her that she has coped well.

MAKING A BIRTHPLAN

Most women form a general idea about the sort of birth they hope to have by reading books on the subject and talking to other parents, relatives and friends, their partner or GP, midwife or antenatal teacher. Regardless of what other people think, you have to balance out what *you* see as the advantages and disadvantages of the different approaches to labour (see page 84).

Some women prefer the experts to take charge and make most of the decisions, believing that they know best. If this leads to the sort of birth that suits you there's no problem. However, many parents are disappointed because decisions made by other people turn out to be wrong for them. Ideally, you'd discuss your wishes with your midwife beforehand, but it's not always possible in busy hospitals. The midwife you see during pregnancy may not look after you in labour.

A birthplan makes you think about what's important to you. It can make you more realistic about labour, or even prompt you to change your hospital booking (see page 93), as you come to realize that certain things in childbirth go together. For example, it may be easier to achieve a natural birth in a low-tech hospital or at home, as the staff in a high-tech hospital may see the need to use technology – speeding up labour with drugs for instance – where a midwife at a home birth might not consider that it's necessary.

A birthplan conveys your wishes to the staff even if you're too busy coping with contractions to discuss them. Your hospital may provide a form or you could use the birthplan available from the Maternity Alliance (see Appendix). Alternatively, you could simply write a letter that can be attached to your notes, briefly describing the approach that suits you best and specifying three or four things that are really important to you. A birthplan isn't cast in concrete – you can always change your mind later.

There are many ways of giving birth safely. Your midwife will make sure that what you choose is safe, so in the end it comes down to what makes you feel happy and confident, and only you can decide that!

PAIN IN LABOUR

The amount of pain you experience in labour is determined by physical factors such as the shape of your pelvis and the position of your baby, and psychological factors such as fear. You may describe contractions as strong sensation, or you may find them agonizing.

Some women feel daunted by the thought of pain and have an epidural at the earliest opportunity; others accept severe pain in preference to using any drugs. Being realistic, and able to relax and be positive, raises your pain threshold, and women who attend antenatal classes use fewer drugs for pain relief. They either feel less pain or handle it better. Pain in labour needn't be overwhelming – *you* decide how much you're prepared to tolerate.

* Companions in labour: do you want a friend or relative instead of or in addition to your partner, to share support if labour is long? Do you want your partner to stay throughout labour or to leave during certain procedures? Can he stay for a Caesarean birth?

* Your stay in hospital: do you want to know the midwife who delivers you, do you prefer to be examined by a female doctor, or do you have special needs because of a disability, a language difficulty, your religion or diet? Do you mind students being present during labour and delivery? Enemas are rarely offered but you can ask for one if your bowel is full.

* Positions for labour and delivery (see pages 112-15): upright positions work with gravity; they tend to speed labour up and help you push, but you may get tired. Lying down lets you rest but may prolong labour.

* Pain relief: pethidine and epidurals help severe pain but may have some side effects and it may be hard to move about or change position. Gas and air, TENS, and self-help methods do not affect your baby but are only effective for moderate pain. If you prefer not to use drugs you could ask the staff for help and support.

* Speeding up labour: breaking the waters (see page 147) may shorten labour, although it may be more intense and require more pain relief. If it fails a hormone drip (see page 146-7) may be needed. This also shortens labour but your baby may become distressed so you'll be continuously monitored and movement may be restricted. If this fails you might need a Caesarean section.

* Monitoring the baby by machine (see page 148): having a continuous record of your baby's heartbeat may give you confidence, but the trace can be hard to interpret, leading to unnecessary anxiety or intervention. Belt monitors restrict your movement; scalp electrodes allow more movement but are also invasive.

* Episiotomy or tear (see page 151): an episiotomy could be bigger than a tear but neater to repair. Women who express a strong desire not to have either are more likely to achieve their wish!

* Delivery of placenta (see page 138): Leaving the cord to pulsate may mean up to an hour's wait for the placenta, but the baby gets extra blood and a gentler transition to independent breathing. Having an injection reduces bleeding and brings the placenta away quickly but the cord must be cut immediately. Say if you prefer a 'gentle birth' (see page 137).

* After the birth: do you prefer to hold your baby immediately or after she's been cleaned and wrapped up? Do you want to breastfeed immediately? Would you like to have a bath with your partner and baby shortly after the birth.

Self-help methods of pain relief

Most people learn to handle moderate pain in everyday life, for example by simply ignoring a headache or using a hot water bottle for stomach ache. *Distraction, temperature changes, movement* and *touch* are thought to work by stimulating larger nerve bundles which, like shutting gates, intercept pain messages as they travel along fine nerves to the brain. When your body gets used to the stimulus you feel pain again as the gates swing open but changing the stimulus shuts them again. This principle can help you cope with labour pain. Try these self-help methods:

Problem: In early labour your contractions hurt and you feel apprehensive.

Self-help: *Distraction*: watch TV or a video, beat your partner at Scrabble, or sort through the family photos.

Problem: Your stomach aches during or between contractions.

Self-help: *Touch*: massage under your bump with a relaxed hand; *warmth*: use a hot water bottle wrapped in a towel; *movement*: change position and rock your pelvis gently.

Problem: You have constant backache, peaking at each contraction.

Self-help: *Change the temperature*: press your back to the central heating radiator padded with a towel, use a flannel wrung out in iced water, or a packet of frozen peas wrapped in a towel; *touch*: ask your partner to massage your back.

Problem: Contractions are overwhelmingly strong.

Self-help: *Focussing*: ask your partner to count slowly through each contraction with you; *movement*: rotate your pelvis gently, change your position, rock your body, make yourself walk to the toilet.

__Backache Massage__ Your partner places his hands either side of your spine keeping his elbows straight while he applies pressure.

Alternatively, you may find it comfortable to stand with your feet apart, leaning onto the bed or another piece of furniture.

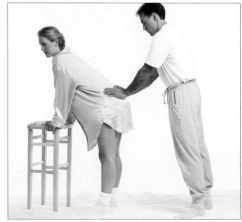

Backache massage in labour

Firm massage or pressure can help if you feel the contractions in your back. Your partner should use body weight, not muscle power, so that he can keep it up for as long as necessary. Use talc or oil to prevent soreness and tell him the best position – usually it's about halfway between the base of your spine and your waist. Practise beforehand the techniques on page 120 and below.

Your partner supports himself on his hands and presses the balls of his feet against your spine.

Sit or lie with the base of your spine against your partner's, while he leans gently back to apply pressure.

Your partner supports his elbow on his hip bone, leaning gently forwards. It may be easier if his body is at an angle.

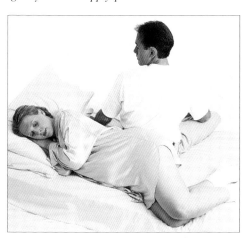

Other methods of pain relief

Each method of pain relief has advantages and disadvantages. For example, gas and air has little effect on your baby but may only relieve moderate pain. Pethidine and epidurals are effective for severe pain, but against this you have to balance their potential side effects. Think about it beforehand, but choose the most appropriate method of relief available at the time.

Epidural: A pain relieving drug is passed through a fine tube into the space around your spinal cord, eliminating sensation in your tummy. It can be topped up as needed. You may have a drip to accelerate labour and counter-act low blood pressure, a monitor for your baby's heartbeat and a catheter in your bladder. About half of all women who have epidurals need an episiotomy and an assisted delivery (see pages 149-51). Occasionally women who have an epidural get severe headaches afterwards. Research evidence is conflicting as to whether more women suffer long term backache. However, an epidural is the most effective method of relief for severe pain.

Pethidine: This is given by injection, once or more during labour. If you are small, a vegetarian or someone who rarely takes medicines or alcohol, a small dose may be adequate. You'll stay in bed as it makes you drowsy; most women say it distances the pain rather than taking it away. Women react differently and some suffer nausea or vomiting, but another drug can stop this. If you have pethidine too close to delivery your baby may need an antidote or be sleepy, so that breastfeeding is difficult at first. Against this, pethidine is a muscle relaxant and helps relieve severe pain.

Gas and air (Entonox): You inhale a mixture of nitrous oxide and oxygen through a face mask or mouth piece. It makes you feel light-headed, rather like having three sherries on an empty stomach. If you don't like the sensation just stop taking it! The secret of using it successfully lies in timing. Take deep breaths at the start of a contraction so that it takes effect at its height. If you wait until the contraction hurts it's too late; you'll get pain relief between contractions, not during them.

TENS: Transcutaneous electrical nerve stimulation consists of a battery-powered device with electrodes that are taped to specific areas of your back. At low frequencies it helps release endorphins, your body's natural pain-killers, while at higher levels it stops pain messages reaching the brain. The frequency can be increased as your contractions become stronger. Some women say TENS feels tingly, like fine sand paper rubbed on your skin. Practise beforehand to get used to the sensa-

'It's surprising how much you can decide for yourself in labour. I want to move around so I hope I don't need pethidine or an epidural. I don't fancy a crowd of students coming in to gawp at the last minute, but they have to learn so I wrote on my birthplan that I prefer a student to be there the whole time. The most important thing is to have my baby with me after the birth, not taken off to some nursery, because as I'm partially deaf I'd worry about not hearing her if she cries. ' JUSTINE

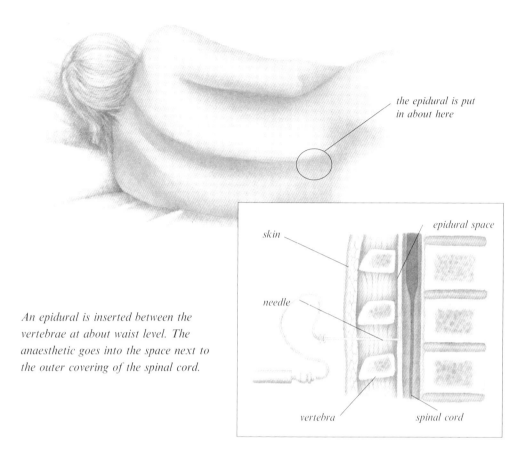

the epidural is put in about here

skin

epidural space

needle

An epidural is inserted between the vertebrae at about waist level. The anaesthetic goes into the space next to the outer covering of the spinal cord.

vertebra

spinal cord

tion, but if you don't like it you can take it off. You can't have a bath, but your partner can massage you without removing the electrodes. The hospital may lend you a machine, or you can arrange to hire one.

Acupuncture, Electro-acupuncture and Acupressure: Needles, electrical stimulation and pressure (respectively) can reduce pain when applied to specific points in the body. In labour you may be able to use electro-acupuncture or acupressure yourself. Acupuncture requires the presence of a specialist, and treatment may begin before the birth.

Hypnosis: Most antenatal classes teach some form of relaxation technique. The hypnotist takes this to a deeper level and helps you to narrow your attention until you are ready to accept the suggestion that you will feel no pain during labour. The hypnotherapist may be present during labour, or you may learn self-hypnosis or auto-suggestion. Several sessions are needed, starting some weeks before the birth. Hypnosis may work by altering your emotional response to pain. Only about 25 per cent of women can be fully hypnotized, but others may find some help from the technique.

HOME PLANNER

◆ *Arrange for someone to feed any pets at home while you're in labour.*

◆ *Remember to stock up the freezer, buy tins/packets for the early days.*

◆ *Stock up on household basics like detergent, biscuits for visitors, extra food, soap etc if relatives are staying.*

◆ *Buy batteries for a cassette recorder, film for a camera, thank-you notes and small surprises to keep toddlers occupied.*

◆ *Pack a bag if your toddler is going away; write a diary of her day to help whoever looks after her.*

◆ *List phone numbers – midwife, GP, hospital, partner, friends, neighbours, relatives – on a pinboard and write down all offers of help!*

QUESTIONS AND ANSWERS

Q: I want to use upright positions in labour. Is there a new sort of epidural where you can walk about instead of having to lie in bed all the time?

A: Several hospitals offer mobile epidurals, a combination of a spinal block (similar to an epidural but placed lower down the back) and a conventional epidural. At present they are not widely available as they are still being evaluated. They are given in the same way as ordinary epidurals and can be topped up. Less anaesthetic is used but they have similar disavantages to ordinary epidurals. The anaesthetist makes sure that you have full use of your legs before letting you walk about. On the whole women like them, although some do not get full mobility. The Research and Information Group of the NCT (see Appendix) are interested in hearing about women's experiences of mobile epidurals.

Q: I assumed my husband would be with me at the birth but to my dismay he has suddenly refused. I feel rejected and worried about coping alone. How can I persuade him to change his mind?

A: Twenty-five years ago few fathers were present when their children were born. Today most men are there, a revolution that is bound to suit some people better than others.

If he refused because he's anxious about his role, finding out how to help you may be the answer. But some men simply don't want to witness labour and delivery and this attitude isn't a betrayal. Relationships work in different ways and there's more to being a good husband or father than attending the birth!

You won't be alone when your baby is born. Your midwife will provide some help and companionship as part of her professional duties. Single mothers or women whose partners work away often ask a close relative or girlfriend to be their birth partner. Why not consider this? It's a privilege for the person you choose and it can also be great fun. She can attend antenatal classes with you and share your experience in a way that complements your husband's involvement. If he feels there is no pressure on him you may find your husband's feelings change and he wants to be more actively involved, perhaps staying for the early part of your labour. You might even end up with two birth partners working together!

Q: I am determined to avoid stitches after the birth and have heard that massaging the tissue around the vagina can help. How should I do this?

A: Nobody can guarantee that you won't need stitches because it depends to some extent on factors like your baby's position and whether the delivery needs assistance. However, you can help to avoid damage to your perineum (the tissue between the vagina and anus) by gently massaging it.

In the last few weeks of pregnancy massage vitamin E or wheatgerm oil (these are particularly suitable although any pure vegetable oil would do) into your perineum for about five minutes each day. Immediately after your bath is a good time. When it's completely absorbed, gently stretch the tissue with your fingers until you feel a slight burning sensation.

In time you'll find your perineum stretches further before you feel this sensation, proving that it's becoming more supple and less likely to be damaged during the birth. When you are in labour, ask your midwife to help you to avoid the need for any stitches, or write this on your birthplan (see page 118).

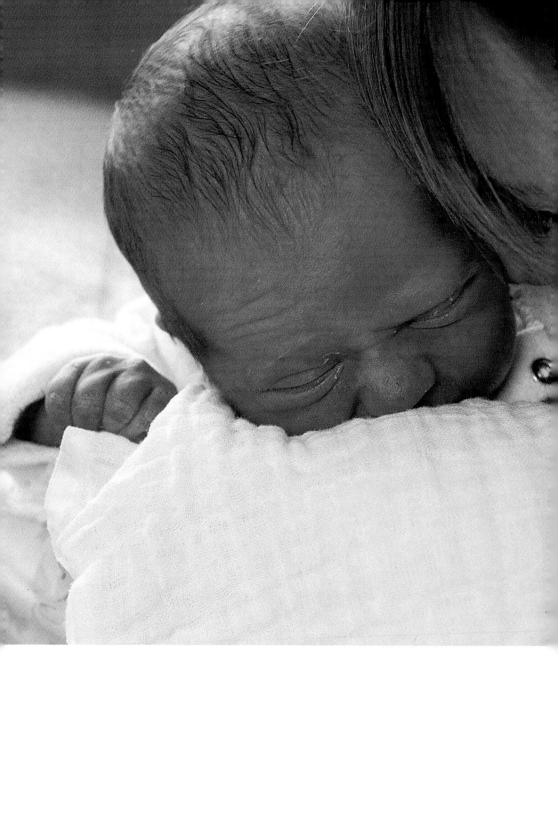

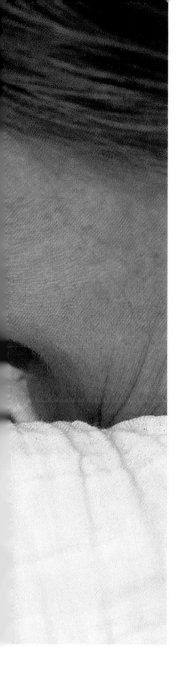

9

Labour and Birth

❛ *When my contractions started it felt like being launched into space for the first time. I bubbled with excitement and elation and couldn't wait to see my baby but at the same time I was terrified! After all the theory and the preparations I had to jump and trust that I could fly.* ❜

WHEN WILL THE BABY ARRIVE?

About 85 per cent of babies are born within two weeks either side of their due date. When this date is calculated from the first day of your last period, some 10 per cent (mostly first babies) go two weeks overdue. When it is estimated by ultrasound scan only about two per cent arrive two weeks late.

The timing of labour may be inherited from your baby's father, as some women go into labour consistently early with one partner but become overdue with a new partner. His family may be a better guide to whether your baby will be born on time than your own family, although babies do mature at different rates and tend to come when they're ready!

If you notice signs of labour starting three weeks or more before your due date, seek help straight away. Many babies come early without problems, but some will need specialist help. If you have several weeks to go the hospital may try to delay your labour to give your baby more time to mature. Take your notes with you when you stay away from home and contact the nearest hospital if labour does start.

If you go a week or more overdue it can be stressful, and after two weeks the hospital may want you to be induced (see page 146). Receiving concerned phone calls and comments from friends or relatives when your due date passes with no signs of labour may make you feel inadequate, like a performing seal who can't perform! On the other hand, the last few days before your baby's birth could be a very special time for you and your partner. Arrange treats or outings to look forward to together instead of just sitting around waiting for contractions.

WHAT CONTRACTIONS FEEL LIKE

If you tense your leg, the muscles in your thigh contract and become hard. When you relax they soften again. You tighten your leg muscles voluntarily but hormones make your uterus contract involuntarily to open your cervix. Your baby's head (or bottom) then holds it open and the next contraction stretches it slightly more. As more hormones are secreted during labour the contractions become stronger, dilating your cervix more effectively.

Did you wonder what the baby's movements would feel like when you were first pregnant, only to find the sensation strangely familiar when you felt it? You may notice the same about your contractions, although women clearly do feel the sensations differently as the following quotes show.

'At first the contractions felt like period pains down at the bottom of my tummy. Then they intensified into a hot sort of cramping sensation. My whole body went rigid with each one.'

'Nobody told me that you sometimes feel the contractions all in your back so it came as a shock. I kept waiting for something to happen in my tummy, but it never did.'

'The sensation started in my back and radiated round to my tummy and down my legs. It felt like the ache you get if you have cramp. I could still feel it when the contraction was over.'

'My contractions felt as if someone was hugging me too tightly so that I couldn't breathe. They weren't very painful but there was this tremendous sensation of pressure that almost overwhelmed me.'

BEFORE LABOUR STARTS

The first stage of labour lasts from when your cervix begins to open until you're fully dilated, ready to push. Before dilating your cervix softens and thins out. Some women experience diarrhoea, or have a 'show' of blood-streaked jelly – enough to cover the top joint of your thumb. This is the mucus plug that seals the cervix and it means that your cervix is softening. If there's fresh bleeding tell your midwife or hospital, but otherwise do nothing. You might not feel contractions for some hours, or even days.

Sometimes the 'waters' leak and you keep finding that your pants are damp; or the waters may break (see page 141). Phone your midwife or the hospital for advice – they will probably want to check you. Even if you have no contractions for several hours they may become strong quite quickly once they start.

Many women have regular contractions as the cervix thins and the baby's head moves deeper into the pelvis. You may feel niggly pains that come and go over several days, or you may have painful tightenings that continue for hours, or even a day. The length and strength of the contractions is usually more significant than the interval between them. If they last 30-40 seconds and you feel normal enough to chat or drink a cup of tea in between them it's unlikely that you're about to give birth, even if they are five minutes apart. Doing something different may make these contractions disappear for a while. Have a bath or go out for a walk if you've been resting, or lie down if you've been up and about.

The 'pre-labour' phase before true labour begins can be tedious. So much the better if you can ignore it for as long as possible. Try the following ways of passing the time:

- Ask a friend to keep you company.
- Hire some videos (and a video recorder if necessary).
- Go for a walk or window shopping.
- Start doing a large jigsaw, reading a new novel, making an outfit for the baby.
- Clean out a cupboard, re-cover the ironing board, bake a cake.
- Address birth announcement cards, write letters or phone friends.
- At night have a bath, a milky drink, a couple of paracetamol tablets, if necessary, and try to sleep to conserve energy.

TIME FOR HOSPITAL OR HELP?

If you have fresh bleeding or your waters break your midwife will probably want to check you out, so phone her or the hospital straight away. With contractions, it's a matter of how you feel. If you're happy and confident that's fine, but don't hesitate to phone if you're worried about anything or just need reassurance that all's well. Ask your community midwife to visit you or phone the labour ward yourself. An experienced midwife can usually tell if you're in labour by just talking to you.

EARLY LABOUR

To decide whether you're really in labour, compare your contractions with the ones you have been having. As they build up in length and strength you'll be more certain that true labour has started. Strong contractions last about 40-60 seconds, come regularly and definitely feel as though they mean business. Some women are elated knowing they're in labour while others get butterflies, as though they have got stage fright.

If you're going to hospital for the birth phone to let them know that you're coming in. Get your partner or a friend to drive you there. When you arrive a midwife will take your details and do the routine checks that you're familiar with from antenatal visits. She may examine you internally to check if your cervix is dilating. If it's still thinning you'll be reassured and sent home or put in an antenatal ward. Don't let this upset you, contractions can sometimes feel more purposeful than they are, even if it's not your first baby.

If you're in labour you'll probably be given a single room and offered a bath or shower. It is not normal practice now to offer an enema unless you ask for one. An electronic fetal monitor may be put on your tummy for half an hour to get a 'base reading' of your baby's normal heartbeat. You and your birth partner will then be left together, with a buzzer to summon help if you need it, and a midwife will pop in from time to time to see how you're getting on. Every three to four hours she may examine you to check dilation. If progress is slow she may suggest breaking your waters or setting up a hormone drip to strengthen the contractions (see page 147). Try not to get disheartened if early labour is rather long-winded.

Here are some ways to pass the time:

- Sort through the family photograph album, look at travel brochures and plan a real or imaginary holiday.
- Give yourself a treat – smooth a luxury cream onto your face, eat Belgian chocolates or use some special massage oil.
- Play story tapes or music, ask your partner to read to you or to give you a shoulder or foot massage.
- Try out different positions for labour (see page 112), remembering that stronger contractions help you make more progress.

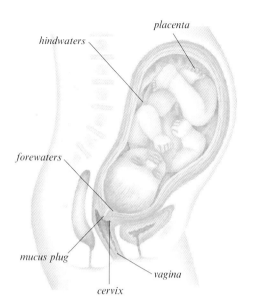

placenta

hindwaters

forewaters

mucus plug

vagina

cervix

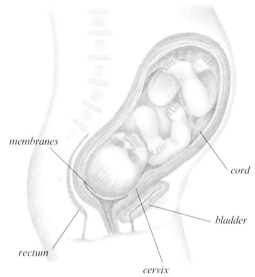

membranes

cord

bladder

rectum

cervix

Pre-labour phase: Before labour begins your contractions draw up your cervix so it becomes shorter and eventually thinner.

First stage of labour: Your uterus tips forwards with each contraction as your cervix opens to let your baby into the birth canal.

ACTIVE LABOUR

As your cervix dilates your contractions will become even longer, stronger and closer together. They may last 60-90 seconds and come every two to four minutes. You'll be making good progress, but you'll probably need to concentrate hard on relaxing both during and between them. You may feel calm and very peaceful; or you may feel weary and anxious to get the birth over.

In the final stages of dilation, or 'transition', there's often almost no space between contractions. Some women feel angry or panicky, or find themselves weeping tears of frustration or despair; others feel deeply calm, confident, and so detached that they actually doze off between contractions.

Your midwife will continue to listen to your baby's heartbeat and make sure you're alright, and she'll offer pain relief if necessary (see pages 122-3). It can be hard to cope with the intensity of active labour, but you're nearing your goal and it's worth remembering that the stronger the contractions the sooner you'll reach it.

' I couldn't decide if I was in labour so we went to hospital when I thought travelling would be uncomfortable if we left it any longer. I had backache all the time, but my partner gave me lots of emotional support. I needed his strength and was glad that he was very firm with me. ' ANGELA

'I didn't realize that labour could go on for over 20 hours. It was much longer and more tiring than I'd expected, but less painful. I only needed gas and air at the end. I tried every position in the book, and some that weren't.

My husband massaged my back and played music tapes for me, but most of all he kept my spirits up. When I was pushing I kept thinking I was going to mess the bed and so I held back when I should have gone for it. But the moment the midwife put Louisa in my arms for the first time it was magical. I forgot all about labour and felt like a star. ' MONIQUE

Be realistic about labour

It's claimed that there are about 150 contractions in the 'average' first labour, while a second or third baby takes about half that number. A text-book first labour lasts about 12 hours, including the delivery but not the pre-labour phase when the cervix is thinning out. So the average rate at which the cervix dilates is 1cm per hour.

Of course, this tells you very little about *your* labour, because women are individuals and are not so conveniently predictable! Some labours start and stop over several days. Some babies take their time to turn to a better position. Some women take many hours to dilate to 4cm and then the uterus gets the hang of it and finishes in less than an hour.

Whether it's your first baby or your fifth, you don't know beforehand what your labour will be like, so be realistic. Some women have an easy time. Others, including well-prepared or experienced women, find themselves struggling for reasons outside anyone's control. Keeping calm and relaxed always helps, but it does not guarantee labour will be normal. Nor is a normal labour necessarily an easy labour.

Accept your labour for what it is, not for what you would like it to be! Midwives can offer help if you need it, so be flexible. Labour will be a positive experience if you feel you made the right decisions in the circumstances.

Most problems in labour are unpleasant rather than dramatic, but nobody can prepare you for a real emergency. It happens rarely and you just have to cope as best you can and rely on the hospital team for help.

COPING WITH CONTRACTIONS

- *Relax with a sigh at the start and end of each contraction.*
- *Breathe slowly and gently, emphasizing the out breath.*
- *Keep checking that your shoulders and jaw are loose.*
- *Rest your palms upwards.*
- *A deep, warm bath may help you to relax.*
- *Using imagery may help. For example, think of feeling heavy and soft, or imagine riding over the contractions on a surf board.*
- *Ask your partner to count aloud to help you to pace yourself through each contraction.*

Long labour

About 80 per cent of first labours are over within 12 hours, without any intervention. A slow labour, although it can be normal, is hard to handle. It can be exhausting and your morale may plummet when there's little progress, but it can also be much gentler and more enjoyable than a very fast labour. These suggestions may help you to cope better:

- Try to deal with each contraction without thinking about those in the past or still to come.
- Walking or squatting often stimulates contractions. Have short rest periods lying down, then get upright and moving again.
- Have several deep, warm baths.
- Go to the toilet every hour to keep your bladder empty.
- Ask for guaranteed privacy for half an hour if hovering staff make you feel tense. Kissing, cuddling and breast stimulation can help to release contracting hormones.
- Send your partner out for 10 minutes of fresh air every hour. He needs energy to keep your morale up.

Backache labour

If your baby faces your tummy rather than your back it's harder for him to pass under your pubic arch during the birth because the shape of his head makes it like an egg trying to fit sideways into an egg cup. About 10 per cent of babies start labour in this position. The contractions turn them gradually into a better position for the birth. This rotation is progress even if you are not dilating, but labour may be longer and pressure may cause severe backache.

Try out these helpful remedies:

- Kneel on all fours, gently rocking your pelvis.
- Massage or have your partner or friend put firm pressure on your back during contractions (see pages 120-1). Some women prefer feather light massage.
- Hot or cold compresses, renewed frequently.
- An epidural if nothing else helps.

Very fast labour

It may seem like a good idea to get labour over and done with in a few hours, but if your cervix opens three times as fast as most women's, your contractions may also seem to be three times as strong! In a very quick labour there may be barely time to catch your breath before the next contraction is upon you. On the other hand, a short labour is usually straightforward.

Some women are disappointed that they were not more in control but felt swept along in a raging torrent unable to do anything but bob about like a cork. You may feel shocked and shaky after such an experience, although you will probably also feel pleased that your labour did not last any longer!

Left: Pushing is hard work but it can also be very satisfying as you are actively helping your baby to be born.

Below: This mother is upright, supported between her partner's knees. As her baby's head emerges the midwife gently guides it to prevent a tear.

THE BIRTH

The second stage of labour lasts from when your cervix is fully dilated until your baby is born. Pushing contractions are shorter and less frequent. They feel different from those that open your cervix. You may think you need to go to the toilet, you may feel a downward movement in your abdomen and pelvic floor, or find yourself making deep sounds in your throat. Your knees may feel weak, or buckle so that you need support.

Press the buzzer if your midwife isn't there. She'll check that your cervix is fully dilated. If you push when there is a rim of cervix in front of the baby's head it could swell like a bruised lip and take longer to dilate. To prevent

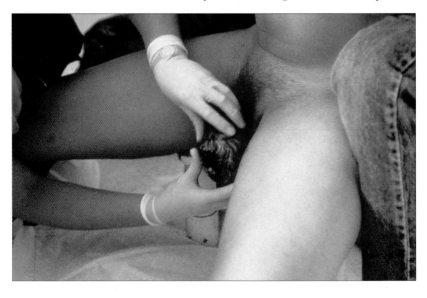

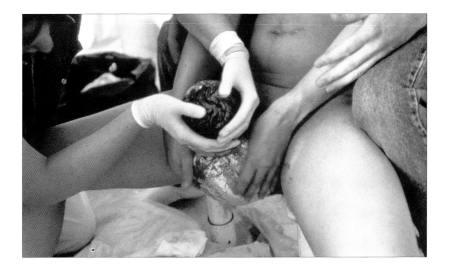

this, use gas and air, or breathe slowly and blow out sharply on each out breath, as though you were blowing a feather off your nose. When you are fully dilated you may need to push immediately or there may be a pause when you can rest. Get into an upright position so that gravity will help your baby move down the birth canal until you get an urge to push.

Your midwife will put on a plastic apron. If you are in hospital she'll bring her trolley of equipment, or move you to a delivery room. She'll stay with you during the birth, guiding you and making sure that your baby is coping well.

Many women find that the pushing action is a welcome relief after the tumult of final dilation, although this depends on the baby's position and

Above: The mother helps to deliver her baby and the midwife supports his head as it turns to let his body slip out easily.

Right: A wonderful reward for all that effort! The mother cuddles her newborn baby for the first time, her face full of love.

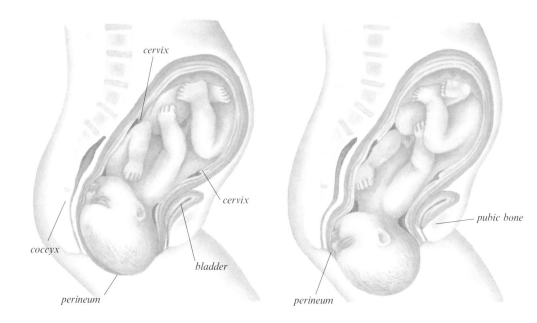

cervix

cervix

pubic bone

coccyx

bladder

perineum

perineum

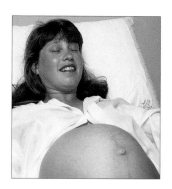

Your baby's head follows the curve of your pelvis, moving your coccyx (tailbone) aside. Notice how thin the perineum is – your midwife may ask you to pant instead of pushing at this point.

Your baby's head flexes up underneath your pubic arch and emerges, releasing pressure on your coccyx and perineum. At this point the back of your baby's head is towards your front and you'll be able to feel his hair.

whether the pelvis is roomy. It can be hard work and you may feel too exhausted to be bothered; alternatively you may feel full of energy, excitement and joy.

Ask beforehand for a midwife who is happy to deliver you in any position. If you choose an upright position, gravity will help your baby to descend, but if the birth seems fast or you've already delivered a baby quickly, you could try lying on your side to slow it down. Ask your midwife to help you to deliver your baby's head without a tear, and listen to her instructions.

Your baby's head will turn to fit under your pubic arch and you may feel a burning sensation as the perineum (tissue around the vagina) stretches. The midwife will support your baby's head to protect your perineum and tell you when to stop pushing and pant instead. She'll perform an episiotomy if

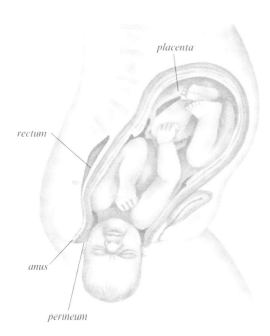

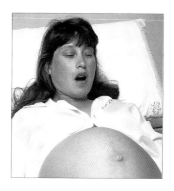

Your baby turns to face your thigh, so that his shoulders fit more easily through your pubic arch and pelvic floor. When his shoulders are born his body tumbles out.

needed. About 25 per cent of women suffer no damage at all or only have a very small tear in the perineum.

You may have an injection to bring the placenta away quickly (see page 155). Your baby's shoulders will turn to fit under your pubic arch and his body will tumble out, to be placed on your tummy or in your arms. He can be cleaned and wrapped up first if you prefer.

Gentle birth

Have you ever thought about what birth feels like for your baby? He's squeezed through your bony pelvis, thrust from warmth and security into space, bright lights and unmuffled sounds.

If the birth is normal, you and your midwife could help make it a gentler experience for your baby.

- Ask your midwife to deliver your baby onto your tummy or into your arms and leave the cord to pulsate before cutting it (see page 138).
- You can provide a particularly soft wrap to keep your baby warm while you cradle him after the birth.
- Ask if the lights can be dimmed and unnecessary noise avoided.
- Bath your baby in warm water soon after the birth.
- If the birth has to be assisted, make up for any distress suffered by you or your baby by being especially gentle and loving with him afterwards.

HELPING WITH THE BIRTH

To actively help the birth of your baby:

◆ *Choose the position that feels best at the time.*

◆ *Think of the entrance to your vagina and direct your pushes down there. Involuntary grunts are normal and can be helpful.*

◆ *Open out your birth canal and 'give' birth. Some women hold back for fear of emptying their bowels, a sensation that's caused by the pressure of the baby's head.*

◆ *Listen to your midwife. She'll guide you and tell you when to stop pushing so that she can ease your baby out gently.*

Your newborn baby

When you see babies with perfectly shaped heads and silk soft skin in film or television dramas, they are usually a few hours or days old! Some truly newborn babies look like that, but others look purple, blue or grey and covered with vernix, a substance that stops the skin becoming waterlogged in the uterus. You may or may not think your baby is beautiful!

Some babies have puffy eyes, blue hands and feet or fine black hair (lanugo) on their bodies. Others have lumps and bumps from the pressure of your pelvis, or streaks of blood from a tear or episiotomy. Don't be alarmed, many babies look vulnerable and birth bruised at first. All this changes quite quickly and in a few hours or days he'll look as perfect as any cherub!

After the birth

The third and final stage of labour is the delivery of the placenta. If you had an injection (see page 155) the midwife will clamp and cut the cord immediately; otherwise she'll wait until it stops pulsating. Your partner can cut the cord if he wishes. Some babies are put on a sloping table to have their airways cleared or are given a whiff of oxygen to help them breathe.

Identity bracelets will be attached to your baby's wrist and ankle and you can cuddle and breastfeed him if you wish.

You may well feel a tremendous elation, a rush of love for this new person and pride in your achievement. You may feel wide awake and full of energy; but it's equally normal to feel curiously detached, rather disappointed in your baby and simply

‘ *Labour wasn't at all what I'd expected. I had a show but then nothing else happened for several days. I had contractions every night and then they'd die away again. After a week of this I couldn't stand it any longer and went to stay at my Mum's house. That night I felt a bit strange. By the time we got to hospital the contractions were so strong that I couldn't walk and they had to bring a wheelchair to take me to the ward. After three quick pushes Kiara was born. I'd go through a birth any day. I can't believe I was so lucky!* ’ DENISE

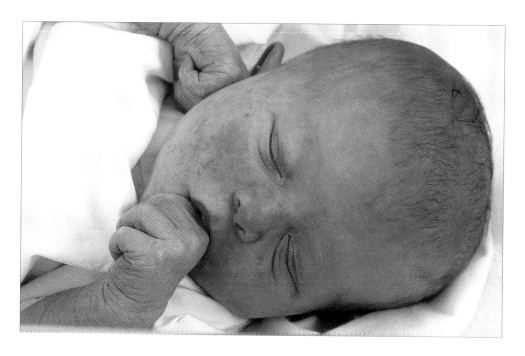

relieved that the birth is over. Don't judge your initial reaction harshly, just accept it for what it is.

You'll be asked to push again to bring the placenta away, although you might not want to! It feels like delivering a blancmange after the firmness of a baby's head. A midwife or doctor will stitch you if necessary, and you can wash or have a bath and put on a clean nightgown. Later, your baby will be weighed, measured and checked by a paediatrician. You and your partner will be offered tea or coffee and left alone to get to know your new arrival.

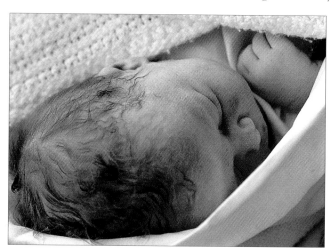

Above: This baby has wrinkled skin and slightly puffy eyes. In a few days he'll fill out and the swelling will subside. His skin is blotchy which is very common in newborn babies.

Left: This newborn has an elongated head. It moulded to this shape to pass more easily through the mother's pelvis, but in a few days it will become round again.

Some hospitals give every baby vitamin K, either orally or by injection, to help prevent a rare disease where the baby's blood fails to clot and bleeding occurs. You may want to discuss this with your midwife before the birth so that you can make a considered decision. Ask the staff to explain the pros and cons of any treatment they suggest, because responsibility for making decisions on your baby's behalf lies with you.

After an hour or two you'll probably be transferred to a postnatal ward and your partner may go home. Hospital routines do vary but the staff will show you the ropes. By now you may be feeling calm and confident like the cat that got the cream; or wobbly and unsure of yourself, like a new girl at school. Remember there's plenty of help available and there's no 'right' or 'wrong' way of caring for a baby. Just give your feelings time to settle down!

The Apgar score

This is a standard method of ensuring that babies who need it receive special attention. One minute after the birth the midwife checks your baby's appearance (colour), pulse (heartbeat), grimace (reflex), activity (muscle tone) and respiration (breathing). Each measure is awarded nought to two points. A total score between seven and ten means your baby is fine. The assessment is repeated five minutes after the birth, and by then a low score has often improved. If the score is still under seven your baby will be watched carefully for a while, but even then most babies turn out to be fine.

Bonding

Babies have no idea of other people's needs and are very demanding. Bonding is the process of emotional attachment that makes parents put their child's needs first. You'll know it's happened when you feel a rush of love, or heart-stopping anxiety, as someone else picks up your child!

Bonding is easier if you can hold and feed your baby soon after the birth, but don't worry if you're separated for some reason. Like falling in love, you may bond instantly or over time. Sooner or later it happens to all parents!

BIRTH AT HOME

If you have your baby at home the birth will proceed much the same as in hospital. Call your midwife when you feel you need her help or reassurance. You'll be free to do what you please and she'll observe you, checking your blood pressure and your baby's heartbeat and examining you occasionally.

After the delivery you'll have a bath while she clears up and collects any washing for your partner to see to later. She'll dispose of the placenta, although some couples prefer to bury it in the garden and plant a tree in the baby's honour. When you're settled and everything is tidy your midwife will leave a phone number in case you need her; she'll return in a few hours.

QUESTIONS AND ANSWERS

Q: I'm prepared to accept pain in order to have a natural labour but I'm no superhero! How can I cope with the pain without using drugs?

A: Try lots of different positions until you find what's most comfortable. For example, kneel on something soft and lean onto a bean bag, or sit back to front on a chair and lean on a pillow placed over the back. Stand with your arms around your partner's neck; rock your body or circle your hips to ease any discomfort. Massage can help: lightly stroke the skin around and under your bump to take away surface tension, or ask your partner to press firmly on your lower back (see pages 120-1). Try sitting in a deep warm bath; some women find it helps if their partner pours cool water over their stomach or down their back during contractions!

Think of contractions as rushes of warmth and energy; or as exhilarating waves that build up, tumble over and recede. Some women imagine riding waves on a surf-board, or climbing a hill and sliding down the other side.

Keep your breathing slow and gentle, emphasizing the out breath and trying to let the contractions flow over you without resistance. Concentrate on relaxing so deeply that you feel as if you are inside a glass ball, aware of what is going on outside but not distracted by it. Remind yourself that the pain is caused not by injury but by muscles working hard to deliver your baby. There are lots of ways to cope and it will not go on for ever!

Q: I'd feel so embarrassed if my waters broke in public. Is it likely and if it happens what should I do?

A: Fewer than 15 per cent of labours start with the waters breaking, and it mostly happens at home where you spend most time. Even if it happens it's unlikely your baby will arrive immediately. If you are upright and your baby's head is engaged gravity makes it act like a cork in a bottle, preventing liquid from escaping.

Put a child's rubber sheet over your mattress for the last month or so of your pregnancy. When you're out, wear a couple of sanitary pads, or even a gel-filled incontinence pad (available from a chemist). You can be sure that if anybody noticed a gush in public (which is rare) they would either look the other way or be concerned to help you out.

Q: Must I wear a hospital gown in labour and can I eat anything? I'm worried about running out of energy if I have a long labour.

A: You may be offered a gown but you can wear what you like in labour. If you're admitted early and want to walk around to get your contractions going, keep your ordinary clothes on. When the contractions become so strong that you want to stay in your room, change into something cool and comfortable like a nightgown, a large T-shirt or one of your partner's shirts. Some women feel best wearing nothing; others feel inhibited if there is a lack of privacy.

In the past women were often only given sips of water or ice chips during labour. When you're in strong labour you may not want to eat. However, withholding food and drink does not guarantee an empty stomach should a general anaesthetic be necessary. If you are hungry have something light such as toast, soup, scrambled eggs, stewed fruit or plain biscuits. Many hospitals provide small meals of this sort to give you energy.

Q: I live an hour's drive from the hospital. My first labour took three hours. What should my husband do if we can't reach the hospital and are alone with our toddler?

A: Set off without delay when you think something is happening, but if there is no time, don't panic! If you are on your way to hospital and you can feel your baby coming your husband should pull over safely and stop the car. At home, he should stay with you, reassure you and use common sense.

Most babies deliver themselves and breathe very competently. They are wet and slippery when they are first born so need to be held firmly and kept warm. If your baby has mucus in his mouth your husband could wipe it away before giving him to you, still attached to the cord, to put to the breast. He could get a blanket to keep both of you warm, and phone for help if there was no time earlier. Your midwife or GP will come immediately to cut the cord and deliver the placenta. Quick births are usually straightforward and toddlers are rarely upset if you stay calm.

Q: I want to have a natural birth but I'm worried that the midwife might not let me. I don't want to be difficult but how can I make sure that I will be allowed to cope with labour my own way?

A: Provided everything is going normally your midwife will probably be happy to go along with your wishes and you should be able to do whatever feels comfortable for you at the time.

Communication can be a problem when you're under stress, so write a birth plan (see page 118), discuss it with your midwife at your next antenatal visit and have it attached to your notes.

Remind the staff that you're keen to have a natural labour when you phone to say you're coming into hospital. Midwives differ in their approach to birth just as mothers do and this gives the staff on duty a chance to assign you a midwife who feels the same as you.

Q: I have had several colds during pregnancy which interfered with my breathing and during a recent bout of 'flu I worried about the birth. What can I do if I go into labour feeling ill?

A: Minor illnesses like colds and 'flu are usually either suppressed during labour or labour is delayed until you have recovered. This also tends to happen with asthma or migraine attacks, sinus headaches and the like. That's not to say that women always feel at their best during labour, but the body seems to decide its priorities instead of overburdening you. If you feel run down or under stress it makes sense to try to improve your general health, perhaps by checking your diet or resting more, so that your body gets a chance to recover its full strength.

Q: I've been to classes and read a lot about labour but I'm not confident that I'll cope when it comes to the real thing. What happens if I can't relax and breathe properly, or if I make a huge fuss?

A: Women often worry that labour is too big a job for them to handle, only to find hidden strengths they never knew they had! Relaxation and gentle breathing will help you to cope with contractions, so they are worth learning. However, there are no rules such as 'you must relax all the way through ... you should not make a noise ... you have to breathe like this or that ...'! You'll automatically give your best, so forget about setting yourself targets. It's not a competition and nobody wins prizes for breathing brilliantly or suffering stoically. All you have to do is let it happen.

Giving birth is more like crossing a field full of molehills than climbing a mountain. You may not know how many there are and some may be harder to get over than others; but if labour is normal the task is not impossible. If it isn't, help is available. Take one contraction at a time, deal with it and let it go. Try to cope not according to any rules but in whatever way feels right and works best for you.

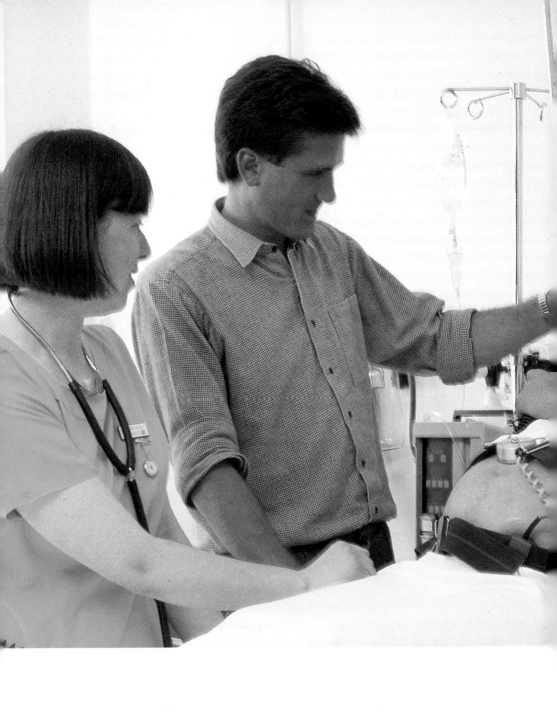

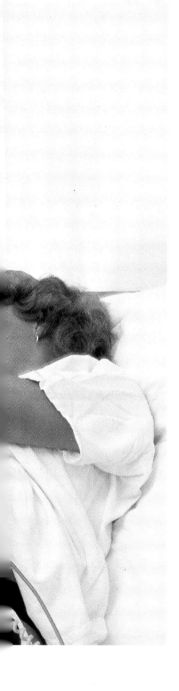

10

Help During and After the Birth

' *You never know what might happen at the birth. Doctors are like the lifeboat – you're glad they're there but you hope they won't be called out! I'm nervous, but I can relax knowing help is always at hand, although it probably won't be needed.* '

HELP IN LABOUR

If things don't go as smoothly as everyone hopes, intervention can make the birth easier or safer for you or your baby. It isn't something to be dreaded; it can provide a positive solution to a problem. Sometimes it is essential because you or your baby are at risk; in any rescue situation you should simply let the staff take control and tell you exactly what to do.

In other cases assistance is not essential but it might help. The decision depends on the professional judgement of the staff (see page 84), and on what *you* feel is best for you and your baby. You could leave it up to the staff, but if you want to share the decision you need to think about the issues.

Intervention usually comes in a 'package'. For example, if your labour is speeded up you will be monitored to make sure the baby copes well, so you may have less freedom to move about and seek comfortable positions; labour may be more painful so you might need more pain relief. If you or your baby are at risk you will want to accept help without question. Thinking about the pros and cons of the various elements of a 'package' will help if you want to share the decision when intervention is optional.

Induction

Labour may be started artificially if your baby is clearly at risk. For example, treatment might fail to improve pre-eclampsia (see page 102), or there might be concern because the baby's normal pattern of movements changes dramatically or she stops growing.

Induction might also be suggested when you are overdue, to reduce the risk of the placenta failing or of a more difficult delivery because your baby is bigger and her bones are less pliable.

You might *want* to be induced, but the procedure carries some risks so the decision should be made individually and only for a good reason.

Some doctors induce women routinely 10-14 days after their due date. Others allow three weeks, so if your baby is kicking happily you could ask whether this would be safe in your case. If you are given a date for induction try gently stimulating your breasts and nipples the day before to increase the release of oxytocin, the hormone that causes contractions. It may just get the labour started!

About one labour in six is induced. Hospital regimes differ, but typically if it's your first baby you'll be asked to go in the previous evening. You'll be examined and a prostin pessary, or some gel, will be inserted in your vagina to soften the neck of the uterus.

Prostin may start your labour easily so that it progresses normally. If not, you may be given further doses at intervals until your cervix starts to dilate. You may experience some colicky 'hormone' pains, especially with higher doses of prostin, and with second or later babies. These usually settle down after an hour or two and true labour contractions are easier to handle. With a second or later baby your cervix may be so thin and soft that it's not necessary to use pessaries or gel.

Your waters may be broken using an amnihook (rather like a plastic crochet hook) or an amnicot (a finger stall with a tiny plastic hook on the end). This shouldn't hurt as there are no nerves in the amniotic sac, but the internal examination may feel uncomfortable. Breaking your waters often establishes effective contractions but if not they will be stimulated using a hormone drip. This will be set up immediately if there is an urgent reason to induce you, such as pre-eclampsia. Where it's less urgent – you're simply overdue, for example – you may be left for a few hours to give labour a chance to establish itself naturally.

Induction does not affect most babies, but you'll be monitored throughout to make sure. If your baby is distressed, a tiny drop of blood may be taken from her scalp and analysed to double check her oxygen levels, and she'll be delivered quickly if necessary.

How painful you find induction depends on how easy it is to establish your contractions. If you're overdue, or have already had a baby, it may be no more than mildly uncomfortable. However, it can be painful if your uterus is not ready for labour. Comfort sometimes has to take second place to your own or your baby's safety, but pain relief will always be available if needed.

Speeding labour up

If your waters break but the contractions still fail to start, or start very slowly, your labour may be speeded up. The risk of infection, which could be serious for a baby, rises slowly after about 12 hours and more rapidly after 24 hours. A compromise has to be reached between leaving the contractions to start or strengthen spontaneously, which could take some hours, and ensuring that your baby is delivered without risking infection.

Sometimes contractions start and stop, or continue for many hours with little progress. Sometimes they are strong but fail to dilate your cervix, although they often become more effective as you relax. Slow labour is tedious but not abnormal in itself; every contraction helps you towards your goal. If your baby is fine you may prefer to accept this pattern of labour.

When labour is accelerated your waters are broken which usually strengthens your contractions. Your baby is monitored and a hormone drip is put into your arm to stimulate stronger contractions; this remains until after your baby is born. Your contractions may be more painful, but labour will be over sooner and you can have pain relief, if necessary. Unless speed is essential, you could ask if the drip can be started slowly and increased gradually to avoid overwhelming you.

Some hospitals offer 'active management' to guarantee that your labour will be over in 12 hours. Once you're in labour your waters are broken and internal examinations are performed every two hours or so to check progress. If

' The birth didn't go remotely as I'd hoped. I had pre-eclampsia so there were drugs to control my blood pressure, a drip to speed up labour and I wasn't allowed to push. They tried to deliver Sam by ventouse followed by forceps. I felt cheated. It was total technology when I wanted a natural birth! If I could do it all over again I'd still prepare in exactly the same way. I understood what was happening so I felt in control. Some decisions were hard to make, but others were very easy. It wasn't a good birth but I coped well and I certainly produced a lovely baby! ' DEBBIE

your cervix dilates slowly a drip is set up and increased until the contractions dilate your cervix at the rate of about 1cm an hour. Your baby is monitored in case she becomes distressed. Recent research suggests that this active management shortens labour by an average of one hour, but does not make an assisted delivery less likely.

Many women have mixed feelings about speeding labour up unless it is essential, so you may want to discuss it first with your midwife. Often it's possible to delay the decision for a few hours, to see how you get on. However, although induction increases the risk that other intervention may be necessary it can also be a safe and speedy solution to a prolonged labour.

Monitoring the baby

During labour the midwife listens to your baby's heart rate through a hand-held or electronic stethoscope. The beat changes as the uterus contracts, returning to normal when the contraction ends and blood flows freely again. If a baby is short of oxygen her heartbeats increase or decrease too much, or return to normal too slowly after a contraction. This gives early warning of distress so that action can be taken straightaway.

An internal or external electronic fetal monitor can give a continuous record of your baby's response to contractions. Most hospitals record a 'base reading' of your baby's heart rate in early labour and fetal monitors are used routinely in 'high-tech' births. They are also used as a safeguard when there is intervention in labour such as a drip, and if there is any concern about your baby's heart rate.

An external monitor has two electrodes, held on your tummy with soft webbing belts. One picks up the strength of the contractions and the other records your baby's heartbeat. The information is fed into a machine with digital and auditory displays (which can be turned off if they worry you), and recorded as a trace. Your movement may be restricted because every time you move your baby also moves so the electrode may need to be repositioned. The monitor could be attached while you sit in a chair and moved each time you want to change position, but it obviously makes it harder to move freely.

An internal monitor provides similar information but an electrode is attached to your baby's scalp through your cervix. Scalp electrodes are less restrictive; if you had backache, for example, you could kneel to have your back massaged. However, many women feel they are intrusive to the baby.

Occasionally they cause minor scratches or hair fails to grow at the spot where the monitor was attached, although this will be unnoticeable when the baby's hair grows thickly.

The trace from a monitor needs skilled interpretation. If it is not absolutely clear whether your baby is distressed and action is required, you could ask for a second opinion. However, if there is a problem with your labour a fetal heart monitor can reassure you and improve safety for your baby.

Forceps or ventouse delivery

Ideally, your baby needs time to gently negotiate the contours of your pelvis, but no great delay during her delivery. Forceps or ventouse (vacuum extraction) can help to ensure that her birth is neither too fast nor too slow.

Forceps are shaped like spoons, curved to fit the birth canal, with different types according to the need. They are lubricated, inserted individually into the vagina and locked together at the handles like old-fashioned salad servers, so that they cradle the baby's head without harming it.

Ventouse or vacuum extraction equipment consists of a cup rather like a large bath plug that fits on the baby's head and a machine that creates suction to hold the cup securely in place.

Ventouse delivery is becoming more popular than forceps (which take up more space) but the decision depends on the actual circumstances and the experience of the doctor. The method he or she feels most confident using is likely to be the most successful.

Your baby might become distressed if the birth is too slow. Normally her head aligns with your pubic arch, moves down the birth canal with each pushing contraction and slips back a little between contractions. Some babies make no progress because they slip back too far after each contraction, or they try to pass under your pubic arch (which is shaped rather like a wishbone) at an angle. Using forceps or a ventouse, the doctor can gently turn your baby's head to fit the arch, or stop her from slipping back after each contraction. If you've been pushing for an hour or two without progress and are exhausted, it's a great relief when such assistance is offered!

Forceps or a ventouse can also help a baby to come out quickly. For example, a baby might be distressed because her cord was compressed or her mother's pelvis was a very tight fit. Adopting a different position or using extra effort might help, but if the distress continued an assisted delivery could solve the problem. A premature or breech baby might be delivered with forceps to guard against too rapid a birth, to protect the baby.

About one birth in ten is assisted, always by a doctor. Most doctors prefer you lying with your feet in stirrups, adjustable canvas slings attached to short poles at the foot of the bed. Your legs will be lifted into stirrups together, not one at a time which could strain your pelvic joints. Relax at the hips and ask the staff to adjust the slings if they are uncomfortable.

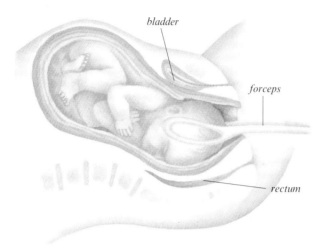

bladder

forceps

rectum

Forceps are curved to fit the pelvis. Without causing damage, they hold the baby's head securely so that the doctor can turn it slightly or stop it from slipping back into the birth canal.

Unless you already have an epidural in place you will be given an injection that numbs the nerves around the birth canal, so that you feel sensation but no pain. An episiotomy is usually performed to enlarge the opening to the birth canal and give the doctor extra room to deliver your baby.

When you feel a contraction or the staff say one is coming, you can help by pushing so that the forceps or ventouse then make it more effective. The doctor uses a slow and steady action, like taking the cork from a bottle of fine wine. A paediatrician will be there, but most babies need no help. You may see pressure marks from forceps or a swelling on your baby's head that

A ventouse or vacuum extractor looks like a shallow cup. It fits onto the crown of the baby's head and is held securely in place by suction. A forceps or ventouse delivery can make a difficult birth easier.

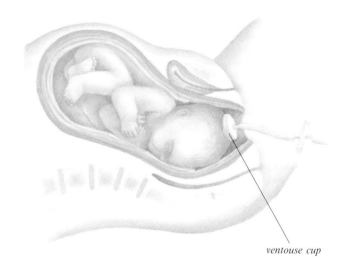

ventouse cup

matches the ventouse cup. These can look alarming at first, but they disappear within a day or two. Long-term problems are very rare because difficult assisted deliveries have been replaced by Caesarean sections. If your baby is irritable for a while as though she has a bit of a headache she will be comforted if you are especially gentle and loving in the early days.

'I handled my contractions using nothing but breathing, but the delivery was difficult. Emily's head kept rocking to and fro under my pubic bone. I tried various positions but ended up with my feet in stirrups. The midwife mentioned getting the doctor, which motivated me to push like mad, but even so I had a ventouse delivery. It was very tense and confusing at the time, but as soon as Emily was born I was euphoric.' JANE

Some assisted deliveries are easy; the baby is simply lifted out, and you may feel little different afterwards from a mother who had a normal delivery. Sadly, others are very hard work for everyone concerned. This is sometimes unavoidable, and you may feel considerably bruised and sore afterwards. You will be grateful that your baby is safe but may also feel distressed at what happened (see page 153), even though it solved a problem and it was not your fault.

Episiotomy

This is a cut made in the outlet of the birth canal, to enlarge the opening and provide extra speed or extra space to deliver a baby safely. You might have one if your baby is breech, premature or in distress, or if you need an assisted delivery. A tear may be smaller and heal faster, but an episiotomy is preferable to a tear that damages the muscles that control your back passage; your midwife will judge this at the time.

An episiotomy is usually performed and stitched afterwards by whoever delivers your baby. Some staff perform more episiotomies than others. Hospitals that set a time limit on how long you can push, or don't encourage you to choose your delivery position, tend to have higher rates. If you use perineal massage (see page 125) and you tell your midwife that you are keen to avoid an episiotomy or a tear, you are less likely to have either.

Although an episiotomy sounds nasty, most women say that they were hardly aware of it at the time. Imagination is often far worse than reality! You may be given a local anaesthetic but in most cases the midwife or doctor waits until a contraction has reached its height. A short cut is made with round-ended scissors, and as the tissue is stretched by your baby's head it is naturally numb.

A local anaesthetic is usually given for stitching the wound, although some staff put the sutures in immediately after the placenta arrives, while the area is still numb, because they feel that the anaesthetic makes the tissues swell and this contributes to later discomfort. There is no need to suffer – just ask for more pain relief if you need it!

'*I had a drip because Thomas was badly positioned and the midwife wanted stronger contractions to help turn him. I pushed for about three hours because he hadn't turned enough. Having an episiotomy and a forceps delivery was a relief. You view everything differently if there's a problem. At that moment I didn't want choice, just a baby!*

Thomas went straightaway to the special care baby unit as he had inhaled something and they wanted to make sure his lungs were alright. He weighed 10 pounds, a giant compared to the tiny premature babies. He looked a fraud being there and he cried so loudly that I was embarrassed! But we were soon out and both were none the worse for wear. ' CAROL

Most women say that the pain of stitches came as a shock. Some discomfort is caused by bruising and swelling, which subsides in a day or two, but you'll feel very sore for a few days and the wound will take about a couple of weeks to heal (see page 175 for ways to cope). Be especially careful about hygiene to avoid any infection. Clean the bath before you use it as well as afterwards, and wipe toilet seats carefully. If your stitches are extremely painful tell your midwife. Stitches inserted after a difficult birth or that become infected can cause more severe pain that lasts much longer.

HELP AFTER THE BIRTH

When your placenta detaches from your uterus after the birth bleeding is inevitable. Heavy bleeding that is difficult to stop (postpartum haemorrhage) can be serious. However, it's not common and when treated promptly is rarely as dangerous as it used to be.

A haemorrhage might occur if the uterus failed to contract properly after the birth because it had been over-stretched by more than one baby, or if labour was prolonged and exhausting, or the mother was weakened by anaemia or illness. The uterus would be massaged and an injection of a drug such as syntocinon or syntometrine would be given to contract it.

An injection of syntometrine is often given routinely as your baby is being born, to reduce the likelihood of excessive bleeding (see page 155). For even faster action, the drug could be given straight into a vein. If the cause of bleeding is an injury to the cervix this would be repaired. Blood clotting agents, intravenous fluids or a transfusion could be given if necessary.

Occasionally, the placenta is not delivered normally after the birth because it is particularly firmly attached to the wall of the uterus. This can happen whether or not the mother has had an injection of syntocinon or syntometrine . A retained placenta is a potential source of heavy bleeding, so you would be taken to the theatre and given a general anaesthetic so that it could be removed successfully.

Any emergency, during labour or after delivery, is frightening for you and your birth partner. Nevertheless, if you have a postpartum haemorrhage the chances of successful treatment nowadays with no after effects are very high.

FEELINGS AFTER THE BIRTH

If you consider the fantastic feat nature performs during birth it's no surprise that a mother or baby sometimes needs a helping hand. It's a relief to come through a difficult situation safely and to know that your baby is alright. Many women can then put the experience in the past and enjoy their baby.

For some women, however, the memory of a birth causes great sadness. This is often linked with the insensitive treatment they've received, lack of support from the hospital team or feelings of powerlessness when events have been taken out of their hands. Some women blame themselves, or feel their body let them down. In reality it was probably nobody's fault – giving birth, especially for the first time, can be difficult sometimes. Flexibility is essential when coping with an unknown experience, but if you wanted a natural labour you will feel upset, even when you know that intervention was unavoidable. Occasionally both fathers and mothers can be haunted by feelings of anger and despair, almost to the point of obsession.

You may feel that it could have been different, that help wasn't needed, or that it should have come sooner. However, any decision has to be made with the information available at the time; judgement without the benefit of hindsight will be fallible. You may feel guilty if you can't come to terms with what happened. Other people often think a healthy baby is all that counts; of course this is important; but it's no compensation for a difficult birth.

Strong emotions are always better brought out into the open and not ignored or buried. You will feel grief at the loss of your expectations, but you have to accept what happened and how you feel about it. Sometimes there is no answer to the questions: 'why did this happen?' or 'why me?' How long it takes to heal, emotionally or physically, depends on the individual. In time you will be able to assign the past to its rightful place and move forward confidently to enjoy the future.

OVERCOMING A DIFFICULT BIRTH

Here are some of the ways parents have found helpful in coming to terms with a difficult experience:

◆ *Talk to your partner or sympathetic friends, until you don't need to talk any more. Find people who will listen to you, not just brush your worries aside or say that what matters is a healthy baby.*

◆ *If you were not able to discuss the birth with the staff involved, make an appointment to do so later. Write down all your questions in advance as it's easy to forget something at the time.*

◆ *Write down your experience, with comments about what made it better or worse. Send a copy to the hospital to help them handle similar situations in the future.*

HELP FOR YOUR BABY

Your baby will go to the special care baby unit (SCBU) if she needs extra attention after the birth. For example, she might be premature or very small; she might have breathing problems after a difficult delivery and need to be observed for a few hours. If she is ill or has a handicap she might need some

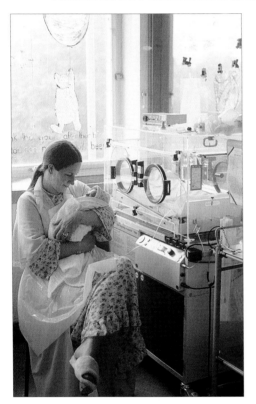

You can often stroke or cuddle your baby even if she has to spend some time in the special care baby unit.

treatment. You will be transferred with her, if necessary, to a centre that can deal with her particular problem.

The machinery and equipment in SCBU can be frightening at first and your baby will look tiny and frail, heightening your feeling of unreality and anxiety. But the tubes and winking lights provide extra security for her, and all the photos of past patients now doing extremely well indicates the success of most treatment.

SCBU is the best place for a baby with a problem. The wards are usually bright and attractive with staff who care deeply about babies and parents. You'll be taken to see your baby as soon as possible (although you may have to sleep in a different ward) and you'll be able to talk to the paediatrician. In some hospitals a polaroid photograph is taken of every baby who needs special care, so that the mother can have it beside her bed to look at between visits. Ask if this is possible; or if you own, or can borrow a video camera, your partner may be able to take a video of your baby so that you can see what she looks like and feel closer to her.

Breast milk is the best food for a baby, especially one in SCBU. Make your wishes known to the staff and ask for any help you need. Depending on the problem involved you may be able to breastfeed normally. If your baby has to be fed by tube you can express your milk. Don't be frightened to do what you can for her yourself, in partnership with the staff. It will help you to feel close to her. She will know she is loved if you touch her, stroke her and talk to her as much as possible.

QUESTIONS AND ANSWERS

Q: I really want to have a natural labour. How do the staff decide when to intervene and what help is needed?

A: A midwife's training and experience tell her when help is needed. For example, she feels your tummy to judge how your baby is lying. If she is unsure she can confirm it once your cervix has started to dilate because your baby's fontanelles (two diamond-shaped soft spots where the skull bones join) are different sizes. She takes your blood pressure and listens to your baby's heartbeat and judges whether they are normal, whether they need watching, or warrant immediate intervention.

If you or your baby were at risk a doctor would decide what action was necessary because midwives generally deal with normal labour. Your consent to treatment would be sought, except in a dire emergency where there is literally no time to spare.

Where intervention might or might not help your midwife may seek a second opinion from a colleague. She should also find out your wishes. Think about the issues beforehand and refer the staff to your birthplan (see page 118) so that you can share the decisions confidently.

Q: Will my partner be allowed to stay with me throughout labour, or will he have to leave the room during internal examinations or if I need a forceps delivery?

A: If your baby is born at home you can have anyone you wish with you in labour. In hospital your partner has no legal right to be present, although it is customary today for men to be welcomed. Most hospitals let you stay together throughout labour, including an assisted delivery or a Caesarean section performed under epidural. Some may ask your partner to leave for examinations, and many will not allow him to be there for a Caesarean section under general anaesthetic. If there is an emergency you will not want to query the rules, but in other circumstances exceptions have been made simply by talking nicely to the staff!

Q: Is it better to have an injection to bring the placenta away quickly, or to leave my baby's cord to pulsate after the birth?

A: To reduce the risk of heavy bleeding, many hospitals prefer to give an injection as soon as your baby's head or first shoulder is born, to contract your uterus quickly. The midwife clamps and cuts the cord immediately and makes sure your baby is breathing. She or a colleague then puts one hand on your tummy and gently pulls the cord to deliver the placenta within about ten minutes. There is some evidence that having the injection reduces the amount of bleeding after the birth.

When the cord is left to pulsate a jelly-like substance inside it swells up to cut off the blood flow. While this happens the baby gets oxygen and extra blood through the cord and there is less haste to encourage independent breathing. Some women prefer the more relaxed pace of such a delivery. If your labour has been completely natural (without drugs or other intervention), and your midwife is skilled and confident at delivering the placenta naturally, it is likely to be safe. Bleeding occasionally happens unexpectedly and rapidly, but if this occurs a drug to control it can be given, directly into a vein if necessary. However, without the injection you may have to wait considerably longer for the placenta to come away.

Further research is being carried out to find out more about the risks and benefits of these two approaches to delivering the placenta. In the meantime, discuss it with your midwife.

Q: My older brother has no sensation down one side of his face and my mother said it was caused by forceps when he was born. I'm afraid of this, so what should I do if I need a forceps delivery?

A: How easy it is for a throwaway comment to make such a lasting impression! Your mother's forceps delivery would have been necessary to solve a problem at the time, and unfortunately the way they were used at that time sometimes caused minor nerve damage. Twenty or thirty years ago forceps deliveries were performed in circumstances where today a Caesarean section would be performed as it is now safer.

Forceps are usually only used today for a simple 'lift out', when a baby is well down the birth canal. Talk to your midwife about your fears. She may suggest writing on your birth plan (see page 118) that you prefer a ventouse delivery if possible.

The best way not to need an assisted delivery is to be well prepared for labour. Learn to relax and handle labour without unnecessary stress and choose positions that work with rather than against gravity. However, anyone might need help if the baby is in an awkward position or labour is excessively long. Try to look on it positively; if you need an assisted delivery it will help you or your baby.

Q: My friend's baby had to go to the special care baby unit after he was born because he had inhaled something and his cord was wrapped twice around his neck. He's absolutely fine now but I'm worried about the same thing happening to me.

A: Your friend's baby probably inhaled meconium, the sterile, tarry substance that fills the fetus's intestines before birth. If a baby becomes distressed meconium is often released into the amniotic fluid. It can irritate the lungs and cause breathing problems if the baby inhales it, although in practice most babies don't.

Many babies with a long cord are born with it around their neck. The umbilical cord is said to be the part of the human body with the greatest variation – measuring from just a few inches to over 4ft (125cm), although the average is about 24in (60cm). The midwife checks for the cord during delivery, looping it over the baby's head or clamping and cutting it immediately to release it if necessary.

Often the baby seems untroubled by having the cord around his neck, even if there is more than one loop. This is probably because the blood pumping through the cord prevents it from pulling tight. However, some babies need extra oxygen or other care, and others are not interested in feeding immediately but prefer to wait a while, to get their breath back. Most babies do not need special care; your friend's baby may have gone to SCBU for a combination of factors, but the main thing is that he's fine now!

Q: I'm having my first baby at home with a midwife I really like. If I have to go to hospital because a problem arises will the staff blame me for wanting a home birth?

A: It won't be your fault if a problem arises! It could happen in any labour, but it's less likely if you're relaxed and confident. Presumably you chose to have your baby at home because you feel more at ease there, with a midwife you know and trust. These things are important for many women.

If you need help your midwife will take you to hospital and she'll probably stay with you until your baby is born. She'll know the staff and they'll be aware of your disappointment that the birth hasn't worked out the way you'd hoped. Everyone will work together to support you through a difficult time.

Afterwards you'll need time to come to terms with the experience – sometimes several weeks or months if it was very traumatic. It's unpleasant to be moved during labour but women who have experienced it say they are glad they spent part of their labour at home; most would have a home birth again.

11

Special Situations

'As soon as the twins were born I forgot everything that had gone before. It didn't matter what labour was like. Their little heads rested on my chest and I was aware only of a feeling of great peace.'

TWINS OR MORE

There are twice as many multiple births today as there were a generation ago, and they are safer because most are diagnosed early by scan. With good care and attention over 90 per cent of twins are born healthy.

If you find out that you're expecting more than one baby make sure that you eat well. Small, frequent meals may be more comfortable in later months and some doctors will prescribe vitamins and minerals. You'll need extra rest, too, and may be advised to leave work early or to get help if you have other children. Pregnancy may be more uncomfortable but unless it's complicated you'll be treated much the same as anyone else, although you may have more antenatal checks.

Many twins are delivered vaginally without complications. Both babies will be continuously monitored and the second twin usually arrives within 20 minutes of the first. If a problem occurs an assisted delivery (see page 149) or a Caesarean section might be necessary even if the first baby has been born normally. Multiple births other than twins are usually by Caesarean section.

BREECH BABIES

Breech babies sit upright in the uterus rather than adopting a head-down position. About one baby in four is breech at 28 weeks, but only one in 40 at birth. Most have turned round by 36 weeks (see page 106).

A breech baby poses simple, mechanical problems at the birth. Usually a baby's head, his largest part, passes through the pelvis and birth canal first. He gets oxygen through his cord until his head and chest are born and he can breathe. The rest of his body, being smaller, slips out easily.

If his bottom emerges first his cord is compressed (reducing his oxygen supply) while his head passes through your pelvis. There must always be plenty of room for his head to follow his body easily as he relies on oxygen from his cord until his head is born and he can breathe. If your pelvis is roomy and your baby is small and well-positioned there is unlikely to be any delay during the delivery. Otherwise a Caesarean section is preferable to risking a vaginal delivery that might cause him distress.

Some doctors use X-rays or CT (computerised termography – a sophisticated X-ray) scans to help judge the chances of a trouble-free delivery. A pelvic diameter of 11cm might be considered adequate if your baby is small; a big baby would need

‘ The staff at the hospital were laid back about a breech birth and made me feel really safe. I had an epidural for high blood pressure which would have been topped up if I needed a Caesarean, but there were no problems. It was a lovely birth.

They put a mirror where I could see to help me push and the registrar just ran his finger around Jessie's head as she was born. My boyfriend kept me calm and the staff made a fuss of me and told me what was happening so I trusted them fully. ’ LOUISE

extra room. A scan may be performed before or during early labour to determine your baby's exact position, and you may be induced (see page 146) around your due date so that your baby's head is still soft enough to fit easily through your pelvis.

A baby's bottom does not fill the pelvis, so go straight to hospital if your waters break. There's a tiny risk that the cord will be washed down first and get squashed, leaving your baby short of oxygen.

'I wrote a birthplan before my Caesarean section, asking the staff to talk to me during the operation and to help me breastfeed immediately after the birth. The operation was complicated and I was very frightened, but even so the doctors stuck to my requests. Looking back, I wouldn't have changed anything. It was an intensely personal experience for me and my husband. We learned a lot about ourselves.' JENNIE

In hospital you'll have blood taken for cross matching and a drip or a tube inserted for fluids, saving precious moments in an emergency. Your baby may be monitored continuously (see page 148). Some breech babies pass meconium, the tarry substance from the gut. This is usually no cause for concern.

You may have more examinations to check dilation during a breech labour as your baby's bottom may slip through your partly dilated cervix, making you want to push too soon. Some doctors suggest an epidural to reduce this urge. Alternatively, you could use gas and air, kneel with your chin on your chest so that gravity takes your baby away from your cervix, or slowly and sharply blow out as you would candles on a cake, one by one in your imagination to stop yourself pushing too soon.

A breech delivery is usually performed by a registrar, with you lying back with your feet in stirrups. You may be given an episiotomy to create extra room. Some doctors use forceps to deliver the baby's head steadily while others cradle it in their hands to keep it well flexed. Then everything should proceed like any other birth.

CAESAREAN SECTION

Over half of all Caesareans are classed as emergencies, performed because a problem arises during labour, but only about five per cent of problems occur without warning. Usually there's time to explain what's happening and to reassure you. An elective (pre-planned) Caesarean avoids the risk of an emergency arising and in some circumstances this is safer than a normal delivery. The staff can be more relaxed than they could be when responding to a crisis. You can also plan ahead and organize your family.

On average, about 15 per cent of women have Caesarean sections today. If you are under 25 your chances are something like one in seven for a first baby, and one in thirty for later babies. For women over 34 the chances are approximately doubled for a first baby, and trebled for later babies.

One reason for the increase in Caesareans is that the operation is safer than it was. Serious complications are rare and for an elective Caesarean section under epidural the risks are very little higher than for a normal delivery.

The World Health Organization recommends an overall Caesarean section rate of 10-15 per cent. How often they occur at individual hospitals varies considerably. The Health Information Service or AIMS (see Appendix) may be able to help you find out local rates.

If you are worried about having a Caesarean birth discuss the reasons for it with your doctor. Some people feel that anything other than a vaginal birth is second rate, but a Caesarean birth can be a triumph, enabling you to avoid excessive trauma and your baby, who might not otherwise have survived, to be born safely. Here are some reasons why a Caesarean section might be recommended, although not all of them make it essential:

- You make little progress during labour. Your contractions may be long and strong but fail to dilate your cervix, or to move your baby's head down through your pelvis. They might be too weak to be effective, even with the added help of a hormone drip.
- Your baby and your pelvis are the wrong shape or size for each other (cephalopelvic disproportion). Your baby could be too large or your pelvic cavity too small or an unusual shape.
- Your baby becomes distressed and starts to pass meconium (waste products from his gut) into your waters or his heartbeat may be abnormal.
- Your baby is lying breech or transverse (horizontally); or his face instead of the crown of his head is coming first.
- Your placenta lies across the cervix (*placenta praevia*), or detaches from the wall of the uterus (*abruptio placentae*), causing bleeding; or the cord prolapses (slips down in front of the baby).
- You have a pre-existing problem, such as pre-eclampsia, low lying fibroids, diabetes, an active herpes infection, heart or kidney disease, or have had surgery to repair the vagina.
- Your baby is delicate or extra-precious. This might include premature or very small babies, and mothers who have had extensive fertility treatment or lost a previous baby.

A general or local anaesthetic

In an emergency a general anaesthetic is usual as there may not be time to set up an epidural or top up an existing one to the level necessary for surgery. For an elective Caesarean you can usually choose the type of anaesthetic.

An epidural (or spinal block, placed lower down your back) means you'll be awake and can share the birth with your partner. You'll avoid the small risks associated with general anaesthesia, and most mothers say that the delight of having the baby lifted into their arms is well worth the apprehen-

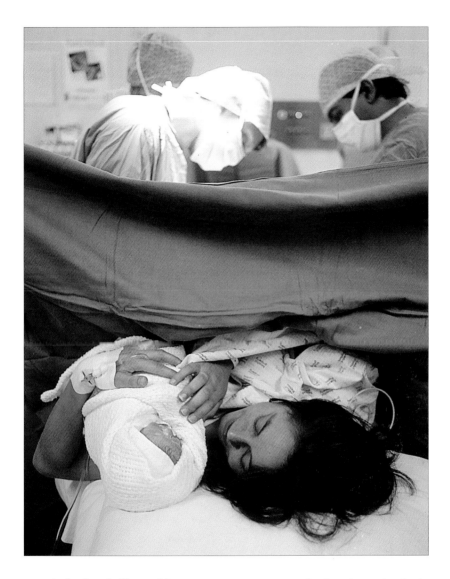

sion beforehand. If a problem arises or you feel at any time that you can't handle the operation you can always opt for a general anaesthetic.

A Caesarean birth under epidural. The baby is given to the mother to cuddle while the wound is repaired.

It is not possible or right for everyone to have an epidural. If you have a general anaesthetic your partner will not be present, but you could ask if the staff could take photos and if he can wait outside the theatre so that your baby can be brought for him to cuddle while your wound is repaired. If he's there when you come round you'll see him and your baby first. Later, you could ask the staff to describe the birth to you.

A Caesarean birth

A registrar usually performs the operation and procedures are similar whether you have a general or local anaesthetic. Typically, for an elective Caesarean you go into hospital the day before so the staff can complete routine tasks like taking blood for cross matching. From midnight you usually have nothing to eat or drink. Before the operation you'll be asked to sign a consent form. You'll also have to remove jewellery (a ring can be taped over), and make up and nail polish so that the anaesthetist can watch your colour during the operation. You'll have an antacid to neutralize your stomach contents, even with an epidural in case you need a general anaesthetic instead.

The top part of your pubic hair is shaved and you have a bath or shower and put on a cotton gown. A drip for intravenous fluids is set up and a catheter inserted to keep your bladder empty. It may be uncomfortable but shouldn't be painful. Electrodes are taped to your chest to monitor your heart and pulse, and a blood pressure cuff is put on your arm. A diathermy plate, part of the equipment used to control bleeding, may be strapped to your leg. Just before the operation you breathe pure oxygen from a mask, for your baby's sake.

An epidural or spinal is set up in the usual way (see page 122). You may wear elastic stockings to help maintain your blood pressure. If your partner is present he sits by your head dressed in a gown. The theatre will be warm so remind him to wear something cool underneath. A frame with sterile drapes is placed over your chest to block your view and the anaesthetist makes sure that your tummy is numb. You won't feel pain but there may be sensations such as the waters being sucked out or tugging as your baby emerges. Sounds such as taps flowing or instruments clattering can be masked if the staff chat to you, or you listen to music.

If you have a general anaesthetic it's fed into your vein; a light one is used for the delivery followed by a deeper one for repairing the wound. As you drift off to sleep a narrow tube is passed into your windpipe and you may be aware of the midwife pressing gently on your throat to stop anything going down the wrong way.

Most babies are delivered through a 4-6in (10-15cm) 'bikini' cut near the pubic hair line. When hair grows back the scar barely shows. A vertical incision may be needed for triplets, a baby in an awkward position, or a dire emergency. Your abdominal muscles are gently parted and your baby is delivered in about 10 minutes. It takes about 45 minutes to close the wound, using individual stitches, a single 'running' stitch, or small metal clips.

' My first Caesarean section was an emergency for failure to progress. An epidural left a "window" of sensation so I had a general anaesthetic. It left me feeling knocked out for a day or two but I got over the operation quicker than some friends got over normal births. After six weeks I was out playing tennis again. ' CLARE

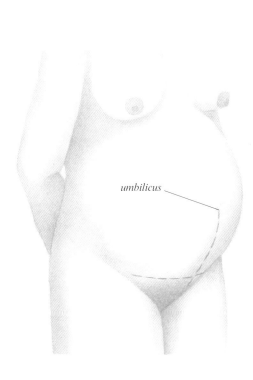

umbilicus

Vertical and 'bikini' cuts (shown) are more common these days. Occasionally a 'classical' cut is made to the side of the umbilicus.

A paediatrician is always present as some babies need temporary help to breathe, although this is less likely if you have had some contractions. If your baby needs extra attention (perhaps for the reason that the operation was needed) you'll be taken to see him in the Special Care Baby Unit (see page 154) as soon as possible. Some hospitals take Polaroid photos to show you your child immediately.

After the birth

If you were fit and healthy before the birth you're likely to recover quickly, although you'll feel a bit wobbly to begin with. General anaesthetics are much lighter these days so you may feel few or no after effects. After an epidural your legs may be numb for several hours. The drip and catheter will remain in place for up to 24 hours after the birth. If a drain was used to remove fluids from the wound it will come out after a day or two. Initially your wound may be covered by a plaster; the clips or stitches will usually come out in about five to seven days.

Pain varies from person to person and can be severe at first, but adequate pain relief will help speed your recovery. You may be given suppositories to help reduce inflammation, plus an injection or an epidural top-up. Some hospitals use patient controlled analgesia (PCA), where you give yourself pain relief through a machine with a device to prevent overdoses. Some women use a TENS machine, or the breathing techniques they learned for labour. In a couple of days paracetamol may be sufficient pain relief. Tell the staff if the pain does not diminish or gets worse, as this could indicate an infection that needs antibiotics.

Moving will be uncomfortable at first but rotate your ankles and tighten and release your pelvic floor as soon as possible. Try not to hold your scar except to cough or sneeze, and remind visitors that laughing hurts!

When you are allowed up, ease your body to the edge of the bed using your arms for support. Lean forward as you stand, taking the weight on your thighs.

‛ Physically I was fine three weeks after my Caesarean, although I got very tired. But psychologically I lost confidence in my body. I couldn't take it for granted any more and was very fearful for about six months. Sex was difficult because I was afraid, and the longer I left it the more of a hurdle it became. I worried about little things and felt I was fussing, but I needed constant reassurance that everything was normal. › JENNIE

Try to walk tall instead of stooping and do not worry about the stitches coming apart – they won't!

An upright chair with arms is easiest to get into and out of and you may want someone with you when you take a shower or bath. The physiotherapist may show you some helpful ways to move. Do as much as possible for yourself, but ask for any help you need and don't expect to do as much as someone who has had a normal delivery.

Caesarean babies are usually prettier looking than vaginally delivered babies as their heads have not been moulded through the pelvis, so that's a bonus! Bonding may happen immediately or it may take time – as with any delivery. Your partner can help you to move, lift your baby, breastfeed and so on, but most of all he can be understanding and supportive if you hit a low patch, as everyone does occasionally.

The first week after any birth is full of emotional ups and downs, with negative feelings mixed up with joy and love for the baby. You may be euphoric because you came through the operation safely, or dismayed that the birth was not what you expected. Your feelings may see-saw wildly, or you may feel very tearful.

Be kind to yourself! Have a good cry if you want one. Rest as much as you can and be patient. A Caesarean birth is no easy option but care and support from the staff and your partner will help you to recover both physically and emotionally.

AFTER THE BIRTH

You may find some of these items useful after a Caesarean birth:
- *Slip-on shoes and slippers – bending is painful at first.*
- *Small foot stool for getting off a high bed.*
- *Earplugs to get some sleep in hospital.*
- *Waist-high pants or boxer shorts that don't rub or irritate the scar. The NCT (see Appendix) sell comfortable stretch briefs.*
- *Fennel or peppermint tea-bags to help combat wind.*
- *High-fibre bran cereal to help prevent constipation.*
- *Wet wipes beside the bed, to freshen up.*
- *A wire coat hanger to retrieve things that roll out of reach.*
- *A soft cushion to protect your scar from the seat belt during the journey home.*

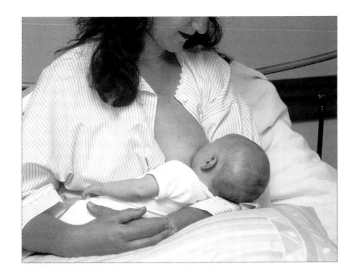

If you breastfeed your baby sitting up, make sure your back is well supported. Put a pillow over your scar and lay your baby on it, holding her close to your breast.

Breastfeeding after a Caesarean section

You'll be able to breastfeed your baby as soon as you feel ready. Anaesthetic drugs cause no problems and the milk usually comes in around the third or fourth day, although sometimes it takes a bit longer. If your baby is sick or premature you might need extra help, but any difficulties are more likely to be linked to the baby than to the birth.

Experiment to find a comfortable feeding position. It may be easiest to have your baby in bed. You'll have to cope with discomfort from your wound, but other women may have painful stitches after an episiotomy. Take it day by day. You may need to ask for help at every feed as you have had major surgery. If you are patient and positive you are almost certain to succeed.

You may feel much more comfortable if you breast-feed your baby in this position. Rest her head on a pillow and tuck her legs under your arms so that her weight doesn't press on your scar.

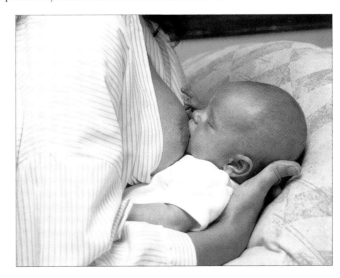

Going home

Most women leave hospital six to eight days after giving birth by Caesarean section. Going home can be unnerving and you may feel especially vulnerable at first. You'll recover faster if you take good care of yourself. Visitors can be tiring when you're recovering from an operation so ask them to come back when you're feeling stronger. There are some ideas for conserving energy below and also on page 177. You'll need extra practical help for several weeks, but by taking life easy most women get over the birth fairly rapidly.

Try to avoid any task that pulls on the scar for four to six weeks. This includes lifting, and driving as you may not be up to coping in an emergency.

The physiotherapist at the hospital will supply suitable postnatal exercises. Start them when you feel ready, but be guided by your body and make sure you don't overtire yourself.

The normal discharge (lochia) lasts from two to six weeks. Some women feel ready to make love after a couple of weeks and others not for several months. It depends on whether your wound has healed, how tired you are and so on. If you adjust your position to avoid pressure on the scar, gentle lovemaking can be more enjoyable than after a normal delivery followed by stitches, but if it hurts you might have a slight infection that needs treatment. If you have attempted intercourse before your postnatal check-up, any difficulties can be discussed with your GP. If not, you can see him or her for advice at any time.

CONSERVING ENERGY AFTER A CAESAREAN

◆ *Delegate as much as possible. If in doubt, don't do something straight-away, put it off until the next day or better still, the following week.*

◆ *Have somewhere for your baby to sleep and a set of nappy changing equipment upstairs and downstairs to save journeys. A table at the right height for nappy changing saves any bending.*

◆ *Have a thermos flask of tea and a snack beside you to keep up your strength, especially if you are breastfeeding.*

◆ *Write down all serious offers of help and suggest specific jobs like vacuuming or taking an older child to playgroup.*

◆ *Stock up your freezer, or buy takeaways or tins for easy meals at first. Check that you have basics such as washing powder, and list other items so that someone can shop for you.*

◆ *Wear loose clothing with large pockets to carry things.*

◆ *Put an advert for a mother's help in your local shop. An extra pair of hands for a few weeks could be well worth the cost, especially if you have other children.*

Getting over a Caesarean birth

Full recovery after a Caesarean birth takes anything between a month and two years, but the average is about six months. Your scar will be red, then pink; finally it will fade to white or silver, possibly remaining numb for several months. However, physical healing is only part of the process. Many women have no problems coming to terms with a Caesarean birth, but others say that the hurt in their body healed faster than the hurt in their heart.

An emergency Caesarean tests your reserves of courage far more than a normal birth. Most women are overwhelmed with fear. Fear does not always disappear once a crisis is over; the reaction can be delayed.

Initial acceptance of a Caesarean section can be a way of coping, like covering your ears while they adjust to a loud noise. You may feel so grateful that you deny sadness about not having a normal delivery until it surfaces later, perhaps when a close friend has a lovely birth. Sometimes it helps to talk about it, to your partner, your midwife or someone who has experienced it (contact the Caesarean Support Network – see Appendix).

Most women need to know the reason for their operation, to view it neither as their body's failure nor as unnecessary interference by the doctors. Try to find out before leaving hospital but if it's not possible make an appointment to see the consultant, however long ago the birth was.

In general it's wise to wait about a year before considering another pregnancy. 'Once a Caesar, always a Caesar' is an old wives' tale! It depends on the circumstances – for example, fetal distress is unlikely to happen twice. Regardless of the reason for their previous operation, more than two-thirds of women go on to have a normal labour. After an uncomplicated operation with a bikini line scar your care next time would probably be little different from any other woman in labour. Discuss it with your consultant, or contact the Caesarean Support Network for advice.

HANDICAP OR LOSS OF A BABY

It's a shock to learn that your baby has a disability. You'll need time to adjust, to find out the extent of the problem, the prognosis and the help available (see Appendix). Most parents want straightforward information even if a definite diagnosis is not available immediately. Many handicaps are not as bad as they seem at first.

If a baby dies you lose your hopes and dreams as well as your child. Such a tragedy can bring very negative emotions. You may feel angry and blame the staff or yourself for what happened, even when it was

' Nobody knows why we lost our baby. It was just one of those things. He'd have been starting school now and I often wonder what he'd have been like. It was dreadful at the time but you come through and learn what really matters in life. You stop worrying about little things. We have two other children and John will always be a precious memory. ' TONI

This lovely baby has had a cleft palate and hair lip repaired. Although it's a shock to learn that your baby is not perfect, many problems such as this can be expertly treated. They're not the disaster they may seem at first!

nobody's fault. You may search endlessly for reasons, and feel guilty about anything from a missed antenatal appointment to simply being too happy.

Grieving is hard work and you'll feel exhausted and overwhelmed by the sadness at first. Later there will be short periods of respite when normal life takes over. These phases will become more frequent and longer, but for months or even years you may find something unexpected will trigger a flood of memories and your sadness will feel as raw as ever.

❛ Joe is my first baby and it was a complete shock to be told that he only had one hand. I felt guilty, even though it probably happened before I knew I was pregnant. I wanted a reason and went through my diary looking for anything that could have caused it. One of the hardest things in the first few days was telling friends, when they were ready with their congratulations.

I wish I could relive the time around the birth. We should have been so happy but we were upset as we didn't realize it would make no difference! Joe has an electronic hand now and he's quite a tomboy. There's nothing he can't do. ❜ JEAN

Some fathers find it hard to talk about the loss of a baby but this doesn't mean they don't care. There is no set way or time to grieve, but you often learn more from coping with sadness than you do from life's joys. If you feel the need to talk several weeks or even months later, when everyone else seems to have moved on, contact one of the organizations in the Appendix.

Life will never be quite the same. Just take one day at a time. Eventually you will come to accept what has happened and move forward again.

QUESTIONS AND ANSWERS

Q: I had a difficult first birth which ended in a Caesarean section, but for my second birth I've been offered a trial of scar. What does this mean?

A: Caesarean births are very safe but in most cases a normal delivery is even safer. Most Caesarean sections are performed for reasons that are not likely to happen a second time. For example, your previous birth may have been difficult because your baby was lying in an awkward position. If this baby is lying well curled up the birth will be much easier, so you'll labour normally but will be carefully monitored to ensure that you make good progress and that your baby copes well. Meanwhile everything will be ready so that there's no delay if another Caesarean section should become necessary, which you'll probably find reassuring.

A normal labour after a Caesarean is called 'trial of scar' because your previous scar could break down, although this is extremely rare if a bikini or vertical cut (see page 165) was made the first time. Occasionally it used to happen after a classical cut, which is seldom necessary these days.

If a woman has not had a Caesarean section but there is some doubt as to whether she will achieve a normal delivery she may be offered a 'trial of labour'. It's the same thing, and doctors often use this term when talking to women who have had a Caesarean.

Q: I have a spinal cord injury and use a wheelchair. Will I have a Caesarean section or a normal birth?

A: You have a good chance of a normal delivery unless there's an obstetric problem unrelated to your disability. If a Caesarean section is recommended make sure you understand the reason for it and feel happy with the decision. Women with disabilities often say that they were not sure why they needed an operation.

Q: My midwife thinks I could have a normal delivery for my breech baby. However, my consultant recommends a Caesarean section. Whose advice should I take?

A: A Caesarean birth is preferable to a difficult breech delivery, so it depends on your individual circumstances. Research suggests that it is not necessary to deliver all breech babies by Caesarean, so ask your consultant why he thinks it's needed in your case. If you feel unhappy about his answer you could ask to be referred for a second opinion to someone who delivers breech babies vaginally unless there's a particular reason not to.

Q: Can my husband stay if I need an emergency Caesarean section?

A: If there is plenty of time and you are having an epidural he could probably be there, but in a dire emergency there might not even be time to explain what is happening. You'd be suddenly surrounded by doctors, whisked dramatically down corridors into the bright lights of the theatre and given a general anaesthetic for speed. Neither you nor your husband would want any delay, but you'd probably be in the recovery room in less than an hour.

12

The Early Days

' *At first I floated about in a dream. Feeding, bathing and changing my baby took up all my attention. As the days passed, the tasks became familiar and comfortable. Within a month I couldn't remember life without a baby to love and care for.* '

HOW YOU MAY FEEL

The days after a baby's birth are heady and exhausting. Excitement and elation may be mixed with bewilderment and frustration as your body under-goes rapid changes and your mind becomes preoccupied with your baby's needs. Take life slowly, give yourself space. Most women feel generally well, but emotional energy can mask physical tiredness. If visitors are overwhelm-ing at the hospital ask them to visit when you get home.

You may feel afterpains for a day or two, a good sign that the uterus is returning to its non-pregnant size. They tend to be more pronounced with second and subsequent babies, and they are usually strongest during breast-feeding; if you prefer not to take paracetamol just relax, breathe gently and focus your attention elsewhere until they pass, as you did during labour.

You will have a discharge of blood and mucus (lochia), like a heavy period at first. It usually contains clots, but if these are larger than a walnut mention it to the midwife. Get out of bed slowly as you may have a sudden gush and feel faint. It is advisable to use sanitary pads rather than tampons to reduce the risk of infection. Breastfeeding helps reduce the flow as the uterus shrinks faster, sealing off the blood vessels. After the first week the lochia becomes pink, then brownish and intermittent for between two and six weeks. Sometimes it lasts longer, but if it's not bright red and does not smell offen-sive it usually tails off eventually with no problem. A heavier flow may occur if you have been doing too much. If you're worried contact your doctor.

It's important to empty your bladder to avoid problems such as infection, but it may be difficult for a day or two. If you can't manage it because of bruis-ing or trauma you may be given a catheter until the problem rights itself.

Your first bowel movement may be uncomfortable, but try not to strain too much. It won't harm any stitches but can lead to haemorrhoids (piles). As your system returns to normal your motions will become softer and easier to pass. Drink plenty of fluids, eat roughage such as muesli, bran or wholemeal bread, move about to tone up your system – and wait. Don't feel under pres-sure to perform – a few days will make no difference and may be nature's way of giving your body time to heal. In the early days it's normal to have:

- Folds of loose skin and quite a 'bump' where your baby used to be. This will shrink and become firmer as the days pass.
- Tiny broken veins, bloodshot eyes, small bruises, piles or an aching pelvis, caused by the effort of pushing.
- Excess perspiration as your body gets rid of extra fluids.
- A feeling of unreality, whether it's your first baby or not.
- Mood swings, or general feelings of inadequacy or anxiety.
- A slightly raised temperature of up to 100°F (38°C) for a few hours around the third or fourth day when your milk comes in.
- Discomfort sitting or walking; soreness and exhaustion, especially if the delivery was difficult.

Coping with sore stitches

You are likely to feel bruised and sore after the birth simply because your tissues have been stretched. If your perineum is undamaged the soreness normally fades in a day or two. Megapulse treatment is offered in some hospitals: the physiotherapist uses a device that passes an electrical pulse over the area to reduce bruising.

A small episiotomy or tear may take up to 10 days to heal; a large episiotomy could take longer. The midwife will check your stitches daily to make sure they are healing normally. Good hygiene is important to avoid infection which would increase discomfort and delay healing. Wash your hands before and after changing sanitary pads and use medical wipes on toilet seats in hospital.

Here are some ways to help yourself:
- Tighten and release your pelvic floor muscles gently to help disperse the swelling.
- Let air circulate around your stitches.
- Stand up to pass urine, so that the flow avoids any sore places.
- Gently wash yourself afterwards to reduce stinging. If you don't have a bidet at home stand in the bath and use a jug or a shower spray (pointing downwards) with warm water. Dry yourself with soft tissues.
- Hold a clean sanitary pad over your stitches to support them when opening your bowels.
- Sit on a thick piece of foam rubber in the bath.
- Put ice cubes in a plastic bag, wrap it in a towel and hold the ice pack on your stitches.
- Stuff one leg of a pair of old tights with something soft and tie it into a ring to make a soft pad to sit on at home; or hire a 'valley cushion' from the NCT (see Appendix) to sit on.
- Ask the midwife to help you to breastfeed lying on your side.
- If your stitches do not feel considerably better after a week to ten days ask your midwife to check them again.

CHECKS FOR YOUR BABY

While you are in hospital a paediatrician will examine your baby thoroughly in your presence. For instance, he'll listen to her heart and make sure her hip joints are stable. He may check the reflexes that help her to adapt to independent life, such as breathing, sucking and swallowing, 'rooting' or searching for the nipple, grasping, 'stepping' when her feet touch a firm surface, and the 'Moro' reflex, where she throws out her arms if she is startled. On the fifth day after delivery a blood sample will be taken from your baby's heel to test for some rare disorders such as phenylketonuria.

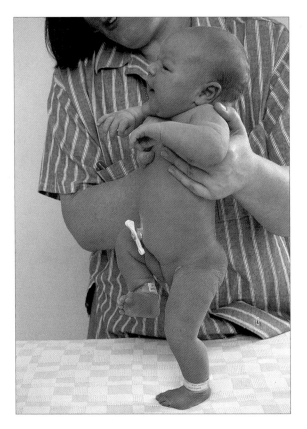

If you hold your newborn baby upright and let her feet come into contact with a firm surface such as a table top, she will lift each leg in turn and place it in front of the other as though she was going for a walk. This 'stepping' reflex is automatic and fades within a week or two of the birth.

Over half of all babies develop jaundice, which gives them a suntanned look caused by bilirubin, a yellowish substance in the blood. Jaundice is usually mild but babies are watched carefully as occasionally it proves more serious. It usually fades after a week, or it may take slightly longer for a premature baby; meanwhile the baby needs frequent feeding. High bilirubin levels can be lowered by phototherapy in hospital under a special light. Your baby's eyes will be covered for protection, but you can remove the blindfold during feeds.

A few babies suffer from low blood sugar (hypoglycaemia). It's more common with low birthweight or premature babies, and where the mother is diabetic or has had a difficult delivery. To avoid your baby becoming limp and apathetic, or alternatively jittery, the staff will want to be sure that she has a good feed within a few hours of birth. Sometimes a baby needs extra feeds, or even a drip.

If you have your baby at home the physical checks will be carried out by your GP, although your baby can be referred to a paediatrician if necessary. Your midwife will take routine blood samples and keep an eye open for things such as jaundice.

GOING HOME

Most mothers normally leave hospital within a day or two of the birth, although you may stay longer if there are any problems. Caring for your baby on your own can seem daunting, but your midwife will visit you for up to 10 days and longer if necessary. When she signs you off your health visitor will take over.

Make rest a high priority for at least 21 days after the birth. You'll want visitors, but the most welcome ones will admire your baby, tell you how clever you are, drop off a little present – and leave! Unless they are genuinely helpful, and you get on very well, having relatives to stay can be rather too much.

' *When Freddie arrived the love I felt for him was indescribable. We are a close family and everyone kept asking me to bring him over and show him off. It was tempting to refuse because he had not been inoculated or he might have caught a cold from one of my nephews or nieces. I had to make myself believe that a cold would not be a disaster.*

It would have been so easy to sit back and tell myself I didn't need my family, but I did; they gave me support and saw the funny side of life when I felt overwhelmed. My older sisters have children and they came up with suggestions I wouldn't have thought of, like not changing his nappy at night because it woke him up and he took another hour to settle again. Everyone threw in advice and I picked the bits I liked. ' LINDA

Although you may feel fine at first you'll soon run out of energy, so rest even if you feel energetic. If you have used up your reserves of emotional energy by trying to do too much something temporary, like your baby waking frequently at night or a minor feeding problem, can get blown up out of all proportion.

Here are some ways to help you avoid exhaustion. (See also page 168 on conserving energy after a Caesarean.)

WAYS TO CONSERVE ENERGY

◆ *Put a notice on the door asking people not to visit between certain times as you will be resting.*

◆ *Don't offer visitors refreshments unless you want them to stay around and chat.*

◆ *Take the phone off the hook when you want to rest or feed your baby. Record an answerphone message giving details of the baby.*

◆ *Make a list of jobs that need doing such as shopping, taking a toddler to the swings, or ironing. When somebody offers to help you'll have an answer ready.*

◆ *Forget the usual chores: grab an extra hour's rest in the morning and in the afternoon when your baby is asleep.*

◆ *Make sure everything (book, drink, remote control for TV) is within reach when your baby finally falls asleep in your arms.*

Most toddlers are naturally gentle with a new brother or sister, taking any unsettled feelings out on Mum or Dad. Try to respond positively when your toddler wants to show affection for the baby.

RELATIONSHIP WITH YOUR PARTNER

A birth of a wanted child touches tender feelings in most men. After such a highly emotional shared experience it may be hard for your partner to leave you in hospital, especially at night if he has to return to an empty house.

If the birth was difficult he will have found it as upsetting as you. He will be relieved that it is over but may feel angry, blaming the staff or the baby for what you went through. He may feel responsible for putting you in the situation and need reassurance to shake off the guilt.

Men are expected to be strong and supportive during and after a birth but many new fathers feel uncertain about their new role. As you adapt to the presence of a precious but demanding baby you'll need to find a new relationship that satisfies both of you. It takes time and can prove stressful.

The early days after a birth are unsettled. Enjoy the elation – it's a very special time in your lives – but be kind to each other, making allowances.

RELATIONSHIP WITH YOUR FAMILY

A new baby subtly changes the relationships within a family, creating aunts and uncles from sisters and brothers, grandmothers and grandfathers from mothers and fathers. It's unrealistic to expect everything to be back to normal after a fortnight!

A toddler needs to get to know his new brother or sister. Small children sometimes behave badly because they are too little to handle the excitement of having a brother or sister, which can be overwhelming. It helps to keep as far as possible to a normal routine. Show that you love and understand your toddler in the few weeks while he is coming to terms with the new arrival.

Babies can unite families very positively. Children from previous marriages are linked by a new baby who is a half-sister or brother to each of them. However, some family relationships may need tactful handling. Older relatives may have more experience of bringing up children but this is *your* child and it's your responsibility and privilege to make the decisions. It costs nothing to smile and thank them for their advice, while you decide whether or not to follow it. Instinct or experimentation will tell you whether something works for you.

CARING FOR YOUR NEW BABY

There is no single 'right' way to bring up a baby and nobody, however experienced, finds what works first time. Most parents use a mixture of guesswork and trial and error, trying different strategies without worrying. However, if you're new to parenthood you may feel more confident following simple guidelines. The first is to collect everything together before you start!

Nappy changes: You'll need a fresh nappy, something to clean your baby's bottom (baby lotion or warm water and cotton wool) and barrier cream.

- Lay your baby on a changing mat or towel.
- Take off the dirty nappy, clean her bottom with the cotton wool and baby lotion or water, dry it carefully and apply barrier cream to help prevent nappy rash.
- Holding her ankles, lift her bottom and slide the fresh nappy underneath.
- Bring it up between her legs and fasten the tabs. If you are using a terry nappy pin it in place and put on plastic pants.
- Put the dirty nappy in a bucket with sterilizing solution, or a polythene bag for disposal.
- Wash your hands thoroughly.
- Babies with very delicate skin sometimes get red, sore looking areas on their bottom. At the first sign of nappy rash, expose your baby to the air as much as possible. For example, lay her on her changing mat in a warm room, leaving her nappy unfastened.

Bathing: New babies don't need bathing every day. You can 'top and tail' your baby, washing just her face, hands and bottom, some days. To bath her you'll need fresh clothes; nappy changing requirements; boiled, cooled water and cotton wool; a soft towel; and soap or baby bath gel if you wish. Fill the bowl or bath with warm water and make sure the room is warm.

- Undress your baby except for her nappy. Wrap her in the towel.
- Wash her face with boiled, cooled water. Wipe each eye from her nose out, using separate cotton wool balls. Dry her face.
- Wash her head, rinse it using the bath water and dry it.
- Take off her nappy and clean her bottom.
- Lift her into the water by slipping your hands under her body and holding her arm and leg so that she is supported on your wrists. Keep an arm under her neck while you rest her legs on the base of the bath. Use the other hand to wash her.
- Slip the hand back under her bottom and hold her leg to lift her out. Dry her carefully. Put on a clean nappy and clothes.

Breastfeeding

Breastfeeding may be simple to establish, or it may be several weeks before you find it easy and rewarding. Babies are individuals: some are eager and can't wait to get at the food, while others fiddle around and seem not to know what's good for them. It helps to breastfeed soon after birth when your baby's sucking reflex is strongest; but if there's a delay or the first feeds do not go smoothly, perseverance and good support usually lead to success.

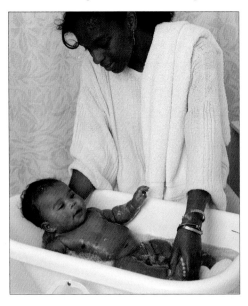

Hold your baby like this when you put her in the bath.

Your midwife will help you with the early feeds. Take your time to find the right position for you. Good positioning helps to avoid sore nipples and allows your baby to take a good feed. It will depend on the shape of your breasts, how big your baby is and what feels comfortable. You should feel relaxed, not hunched up or distracted by discomfort.

Your baby's chest should face yours, with her head tipped back slightly so that her chin is close to your breast and her lips are near your nipple. Chest to chest and chin to breast is easy to remember. Use pillows for extra support if necessary.

HOW TO BREASTFEED

❖ *Support your baby's shoulders and neck with your forearm, cradling her head gently in your other hand. Use whichever hand and arm feels more comfortable.*

❖ *Brush her lips with your nipple until she opens her mouth.*

❖ *Wait until she opens her mouth really wide, like a baby bird. Be patient, this may take several minutes.*

❖ *When her mouth is wide open, bring her head towards your breast so that she takes a good mouthful of breast tissue as well as your nipple.*

❖ *If she is latched on properly her jawbone will move as she sucks. If not, slide a little finger into the corner of her mouth to break her suction. Relax and try again.*

You can help prevent sore nipples by making sure your baby is well supported and latched on properly. Wash your nipples once a day without using soap which removes natural oils and keep them dry. Cotton bras, and the old trick of putting tea-strainers (with the handles removed) over your nipples, can help air circulate. If they become sore expose them to the air as much as possible. Nipple creams may be soothing, although occasionally they also cause soreness. A change of feeding position to even out pressure on the nipple, or temporarily using a nipple shield may help.

Brief feeds as often as your baby will co-operate in the early days will give you both practice. You'll learn the positions that work for you and your baby will learn to latch on and feed well. This helps to minimize engorgement, where the rush of milk coming in on the third or fourth day leads to hard, swollen breasts. If you are engorged, expressing a bit of milk first may make it easier for your baby to latch on. You can encourage the milk to flow by applying warm compresses, or try cold compresses to reduce swelling. Sometimes alternate hot and cold compresses work, and some women swear by wearing a firm, supportive bra with cooling Savoy cabbage leaves inside for a few hours!

If you have any breastfeeding problem ask for support early on. Your midwife, health visitor or another mother who has breastfed successfully may be able to help, or contact one of the groups listed in the Appendix, who are happy to give advice and support.

‘*I lived on excitement after Bianca was born. The birth was lovely and I felt fantastic. I lost weight and everyone said how well I looked, but I wasn't eating enough extra calories for breastfeeding. Bianca was always hungry and I never saw any milk, so she was on a bottle by the time she was six weeks old.*

I suppose I wanted to prove that parenthood was fun and that it didn't need to make any difference to your life. Breastfeeding failed because I did too much. I've learned to be more laid back! ’ *NICKI*

Make sure you are sitting comfortably and that you hold your baby close to your body when you breastfeed.

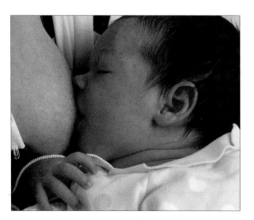

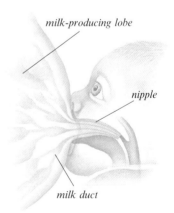

milk-producing lobe

nipple

milk duct

This baby is latched on well, taking a good mouthful of breast with her bottom lip curled back. In this position she has plenty of room to breathe.

When your baby is well positioned, with a good mouthful of breast tissue, your nipple will reach the back of her tongue and palate.

Bottlefeeding

If you are unable to breastfeed or choose to bottlefeed instead there is no reason to feel guilty. It can be a very satisfying experience. Cuddle your baby, and when it's practical open your shirt so that she can feel the warmth of your skin as she feeds.

Some babies like formula straight from the fridge. Others prefer the bottle warmed in a bottle warmer or jug of hot water. Keep the bottle tilted throughout the feed so that the teat stays full of liquid and your baby doesn't suck in air which could give her colic.

'I'd never thought about the intensity of caring for a baby before I had Kathryn. She knows nothing of the world and what I teach her will form the basis for her attitudes in life

I couldn't breastfeed because I had drugs for blood pressure problems, so at first she had bottles. When my milk came in she wouldn't latch on; sometimes she screamed solidly for a couple of hours. It would have been so easy to bottlefeed, but I really wanted her to be breastfed, and in time I succeeded. I was surprised at the warmth she brought from unexpected places. An old friend I'd not seen for years brought me a rose to plant in the garden in her honour. A friend of my mother's sent a little dress. ' ROSEMARY

Hygiene is especially important when you bottlefeed as your baby will not gain the immunities that breastfeeding offers. Germs multiply rapidly in stale milk, so be sure to clean all bottles and teats thoroughly before sterilizing them.

Instructions may vary slightly so read the label on the pack of formula, but in general make up feeds like this:

- Wash your hands and boil enough tap water for the number of bottles you intend to make.
- Cool the water and pour the correct amount into each bottle, using the measuring marks on the side.
- Measure the formula using the scoop provided. Don't pack it down as too much powder can be harmful. Level it off with the back of a knife.
- Add the powder to the bottle, screw on the cap and shake to dissolve it.
- Store bottles in the fridge, but throw away any unused formula after 24 hours.

Enjoy your baby

If you decide for good reasons to bottlefeed you may agonize that your baby will suffer and others may judge you – but other mothers will be busy agonizing over their own supposed failings.

For many years you'll worry about making wrong decisions. Just as you gain confidence in your own sound judgement your children will reach their teens and tell you all over again that you're wrong! Life is for living, mistakes are inevitable – and a mother's place is in the wrong. It's best to accept this basic fact of life early and get on with enjoying your baby.

QUESTIONS AND ANSWERS

Q: My baby is five days old and I'm finding breastfeeding is agony, especially at the start of each feed. I don't want to give up but I've begun to dread it. What am I doing wrong?

A: Some women experience sharp pain at the beginning of a feed, when the milk lets down. It usually disappears after two or three weeks, as the ducts get accustomed to the sudden rush of milk. Anticipate it and deliberately relax your shoulders and take your mind elsewhere for a minute, until it passes.

If pain continues throughout the feed ask your community midwife to check that your baby is latched on well. Don't push your nipple between her lips so that she has to haul herself onto the breast; wait until she opens her mouth wide before you latch her on. She should take a good mouthful of breast with her bottom lip curled back.

Most babies come off the breast by themselves when they have finished feeding but some doze, wake up when they slide off the nipple and then jerk back on for another feed! This can make your nipple sore, so put your baby on your shoulder if you think she has finished. Cuddle her until she settles. Sore nipples usually heal within a day or two once the problem has been identified and solved.

Q: My baby is 10 days old and has had special care since birth. We are ready for discharge now but I'm afraid I won't be able to cope. There's always a midwife to help me here so I feel secure. Breastfeeding still isn't easy. Could I ask to stay longer?

A: It's easy to lose confidence in yourself when your baby needs the care of highly trained professionals, but the staff will reassure you that now she is better you can provide everything she needs to thrive. Breastfeeding is sometimes harder to establish when a baby is ill. With time and patience it will get easier, and when you go home your community midwife or your health visitor will continue to help. Your confidence will quickly return once you find out that you really can cope!

Q: I thought life would be wonderful once my baby arrived, but he's three weeks old and I still feel completely overwhelmed. All he does is howl and I feel trapped. I wanted him so much but now I long to get back to my old life. Do other mothers feel this way, or am I not suited to motherhood?

A: More mothers than you might imagine feel like this at first, but nobody likes to admit it. Try telling your health visitor, or a sympathetic older relative who will understand and support you.

You also need some practical help. It's not your fault that your baby cries so much! Ask a friend or relative to take him out for a walk so that you can have a bath or a rest without worrying about him. Plan an outing on your own leaving your partner to cope at home.

Anyone could feel trapped in your situation but getting out is wonderful for the morale, even if it is only for a couple of hours between feeds! This difficult phase will not last for ever. In time your baby will settle and become more contented and rewarding and you will adjust to your new life and get your energy back. Then you'll find that life with a baby can be fun.

Q: My baby's skin was beautiful when he was born but now I'm home his face is covered with spots. The health visitor didn't seem concerned but was it something I ate?

A: Your baby simply has especially fine, delicate skin, and the spots may come and go for a few weeks until his system matures. They are unlikely to be linked to anything you ate or did. Red spots appear sometimes if a baby becomes overheated and sweaty, but babies who are not too hot also get them. Tiny white spots (milia) are caused by temporary blockage of the glands that secrete sebum to lubricate the skin. They disappear after a few days and you should never squeeze them.

Just when you want your baby to look his best because everybody is coming to admire him, he comes out in spots! They look awful to you, but visitors are more likely to notice his tiny fingers, delicate ears and sweet expressions.

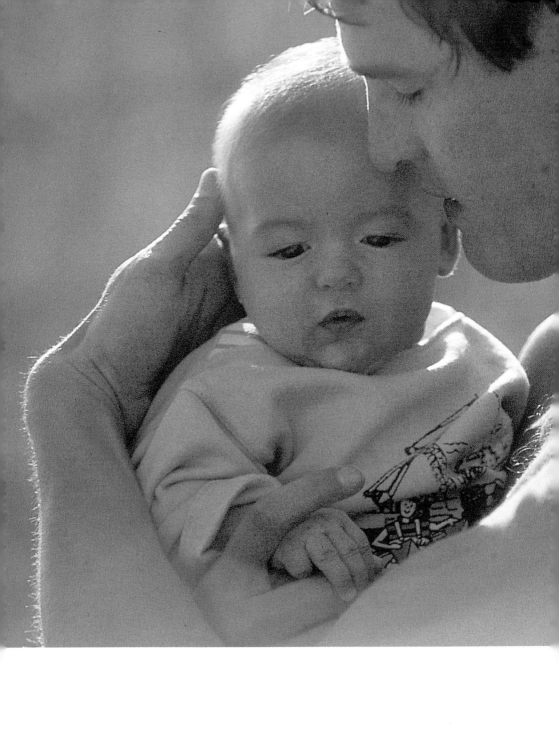

13

Getting Back to Normal

' *I never imagined that parenthood would make me feel so protective. Of course there are bad times when she won't stop screaming and I've really had enough. But then she smiles at me – and I forgive her everything!* '

ADJUSTING TO PARENTHOOD

Parenthood is nothing if not an intense experience. It involves a lot of giving in situations that arouse rather primitive emotions. At times your baby will fascinate and delight you; at other times you'll feel anxious, angry or inadequate. You may worry that his well-being lies largely in your hands and that you'll never be good enough for this responsibility. The ideal of a perfect mother is born of love and raised on other peoples' expectations, but a baby's ever-changing needs make perfection impossible!

Most mothers take several months to organize any sort of normal routine. Congratulate yourself if you manage to achieve one thing per day in addition to baby care. Breastfed babies often want to suckle happily all evening, every evening, and the cumulative lack of sleep sneaks up on you so you may find yourself operating in a daze. Most people believe they need eight hours' sleep every night, but your body will soon adjust to less. You won't feel on top form while this happens, but if you're really exhausted you will probably sleep anytime and anywhere!

For many months ahead you'll be a willing slave to a pint-sized boss. You may long for your baby to sleep to give you a little space of your own – but when he does you'll think about him constantly!

Babies sleep for as long as their body needs and are happy or miserable, according to their temperament. There is little you can do to influence this. If your baby cries despite your efforts to comfort him you may worry that he dislikes you or has failed to bond to you, but it will probably have more to do with his nature than your relationship or how you handle him. Follow his lead until a routine evolves naturally after a few months. When you have a baby your life takes on a slower rhythm. Somewhere within you you'll find the patience to respond to the day to day demands a baby makes, although you may also grieve for a 'lost' part of you – the independent woman who could do what she wanted when she wanted.

If you use a wheelchair or have another disability you may already live at a slower pace, so the change when a baby arrives is not so great. Physically able mothers often have to learn the hard way that rushing about is neither desirable nor comfortable. Slowing down can actually be a source of great vitality. It gives you time to enjoy your baby.

' Before I had Lucien everybody warned me I'd get no sleep. I expected to look like a zombie with matchsticks propping up my eyes, but Lucien fed and went straight down. Everyone said that by the time he was six months old my time would not be my own, but he happily watched me pottering about, or the washing machine going round. I returned to work part time and went on holiday without him and he was fine!

Now I'm pregnant again and the doom-and-gloom brigade are saying. "You won't have another one like Lucien, you know!" The awful things they warned me about never happened, and anyway he wasn't a baby for long. It's best to take each step as it comes and enjoy motherhood. ' YASMIN

Who can help you?

There are many experts, supporters and other parents to help you make the most of parenting:

- Your health visitor can check your baby's growth and discuss immunization, feeding and baby care. She has access to national databases and may be able to help you contact other parents if you have a special situation.
- Relatives and friends can give advice, boost your confidence and look after your baby when you need a break.
- Childcare books can give you information and answer some questions.
- Magazines such as *Practical Parenting* publish informative articles on baby care written by experts. Keep copies for reference as your baby grows.
- The voluntary organizations listed in the Appendix provide a range of services. The Directory of British Organizations (ask at your local library) lists many more groups by subject.
- Your local Citizens' Advice Bureau (see telephone directory) has trained volunteers who give confidential advice on any topic including consumer rights, debt problems and welfare benefits

CRYING BABIES

If your baby cries constantly it's neither your fault nor your sole responsibility. After two or three months he'll be more settled. Meanwhile, here are some things to try that might help:

- Check with your doctor that there's no physical reason for the crying, then stop worrying about this.
- Ask friends and relatives to help by taking your baby out for an hour or two to give you a regular break. This is essential to keep a sense of proportion.
- Take your baby out in the car, or walk around the block. You won't be the only parent to do this in pyjamas at 3am!
- Cranial osteopathy sometimes helps. The British School of Osteopathy (see Appendix) can give advice.
- Contact CRY-SIS (see Appendix) who can put you in touch with a telephone volunteer who has had a similar problem.
- If your baby has colic at roughly the same time every day, accept it and don't plan activities for this time.
- If you think you might harm your baby put her in a safe place such as her cot and go away for ten minutes to calm down; contact the NSPCC Helpline (see Appendix). They will offer practical support, not condemnation.

RELATIONSHIP CHANGES

A small baby changes life for both you and your partner. Here's what some fathers say about their new role:

'It's difficult to reconcile the demands of my job and the desire to be a good father. I'm not always there so I can't slot into Lucy's routine because I don't know what's going on.'

'I love being a father. It's much better for you than four pints of lager and a curry, a pleasure that has had to take a back seat recently! But I worry about my financial responsibility now that Carla isn't working.'

'Ben is growing and changing all the time. I really want to get back to see him each evening, but I feel a bit jealous of the time Abi spends with him. She seems closer to him than to me.'

If you look after your baby most of the time you'll go beyond following general advice (which only works up to a point) and start fine-tuning, adapting subtly to your baby's likes and dislikes. When your partner returns to work he may lose his confidence at baby care through lack of practice. Give him space to find his own ways to cope, without hovering over him or demonstrating your superior skills too readily!

Sadly, the most loving of mothers can be possessive over a baby, while even supportive partners often don't do as much as they think they do. There's a gap between the fantasy of domestic bliss where everyone has their needs met while chores are shared harmoniously, and the reality of family life with a demanding baby and adults who have feelings of power and vulnerability.

Potentially, parenthood means being on call for 24 hours a day with no holidays! Any division of labour is fine provided both partners are happy with the situation. If not, creeping resentment can easily sour your relationship. There can be no change if one partner keeps his or her feelings a secret.

'*Having a baby should change your life, and parenthood is rewarding, but my husband and I found the adjustment wasn't easy. If you want to work things out you really have to communicate. Our relationship has always been good as we had time to spend together.*

When Sophie arrived we couldn't keep up all our activities without getting frazzled, so for six months we decided to concentrate on looking after her and not expect much for ourselves. Every few weeks we made ourselves sit down and set some time aside for each of us. We organized a baby-sitter to spend time together. It sounds very planned but it certainly worked for us. '*JULIA*

Start as you mean to go on: talk to each other and negotiate agreements that suit you both. Close relationships always involve ambivalence, so there will be conflicts. Resolving these through compromise will both challenge and strengthen your partnership.

Your baby should become a happy part of your lives, and not take over completely. After three or four months it's a good idea to sit down with your partner and review the situation. On the opposite page there are some ideas to help you balance everyone's needs.

BALANCING NEEDS

◆ *Time management: some jobs must be done every day; others, such as bathing your baby, could be done less frequently.*

◆ *Weekend lie-in: one partner looks after the baby while the other stays in bed for as long as they like on Saturday morning. On Sunday, reverse the roles.*

◆ *Forward planning: once a month you sit down and plan chores and time off for each partner.*

◆ *Talking time: every week you each spend five minutes listening without interruption while your partner talks and 20 minutes discussing any issues that come up.*

◆ *Regular night off together: you organize a baby-sitter and spend time doing something you both enjoy.*

◆ *Team work: you take turns with other couples or lone parents, looking after the children while the others have a break.*

Your sex life

Some women feel ready to make love again as soon as a week or two after giving birth but most take rather longer. If there has been a lull in your sex life, perhaps starting in late pregnancy and continuing after the birth, you may find that the spontaneity is lost and it is necessary for you and your partner to make a positive decision together to resume sexual relations. Sex may be painful or remind you of a negative birth experience. Full breasts may feel uncomfortable or messy when they leak milk, or you may need reassurance about your appearance. You may be exhausted because your baby does not sleep through the night, or distracted by his demands for attention. You may be so preoccupied with parenting that you forget about your adult relationship. It's not always easy to communicate if guilt or resentment are present, but talking with your partner may help you to find ways to set your sex life on course again.

Discomfort can often be improved by using a different position or a vaginal lubricant from the chemist. Having extra help at home could ensure that you are less tired or that you get a break from your responsibilities. Good humour and a willingness to communicate are essential. Your sex life will be different but it need not be less good; remember that penetrative sex is not the only form of lovemaking – there are many different ways of giving and receiving affection. Stroking, kissing and cuddling are all important ways of demonstrating your love. If you continue to show each other warmth and tenderness, and explore other means of providing each other with erotic pleasure, a full sexual relationship can follow in its own time when you both feel ready for it.

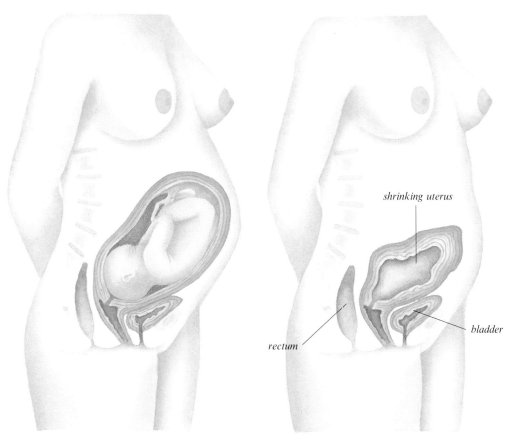

shrinking uterus

rectum

bladder

BEFORE THE BIRTH   AFTER THE BIRTH

YOUR POSTNATAL BODY

Your figure may look much the same as before pregnancy or you may notice some subtle changes. Your uterus will be slightly bigger than previously and your tummy may have a more rounded outline. It will feel flabby at first, becoming firmer after a few weeks. Your breasts may be larger if you are breastfeeding. If not, they'll be smaller and softer for several months while the fatty tissue that shapes them builds up, replacing the milk-producing tissue that developed in pregnancy.

Your pelvic floor is stretched during a normal birth and you may suffer stress incontinence when you cough or laugh. The muscle tone can be improved with pelvic floor exercises (see page 45), but it may be several months before you feel confident again.

The scar from a tear or episiotomy may feel strange and it can be reassuring to take a look using a hand mirror. Your periods might return in a few weeks, or not for a year or more if you are fully breastfeeding. You can conceive

192

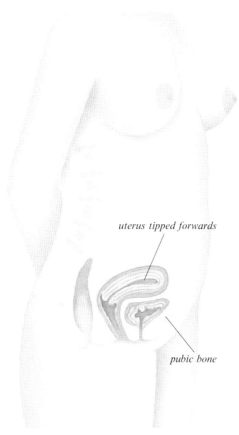

uterus tipped forwards

pubic bone

__Far left:__ Your uterus takes up a lot of room a the end of pregnancy, stretching your abdomen and compressing your internal organs.
__Centre:__ After your baby is born your uterus shrinks rapidly but you'll still look about five to six months pregnant. Your intestines have more room and they'll gradually resume their normal place.
__Left:__ Six weeks after the birth your uterus will have contracted to the size of a small pear and returned to its normal position in your body.

SIX WEEKS LATER

before your first period. Becoming pregnant soon after giving birth could put a strain on your body, so use contraception unless you are sure that you really want another baby immediately.

Some women rapidly return to their pre-pregnancy weight, although this depends on body type. It's unwise to diet while breastfeeding, but after several months you'll naturally lose the extra fat stores laid down during pregnancy. If you bottlefeed and want to lose weight it may be necessary to watch what you eat and take more exercise.

When you're heavily pregnant you can't see over your bump and you may be dismayed to discover stretchmarks. These are red and unsightly at first. There's nothing you can do about them (they depend partly on skin type) but they fade to pink and eventually to a barely noticeable silvery cream.

Some women find their joints ache, especially after lifting or standing too long. Rest more and take care not to strain yourself – they'll stabilize as your hormones settle down.

Back and Buttock Exercise
1. Lie on the floor with your knees raised.

2. Tighten your buttock muscles and lift your hips. Hold for a few seconds, then slowly lower your back down to the floor.

Postnatal exercises

In the early months, general exercise classes may be too strenuous as your ligaments will still be soft and easily strained. Buy a video or find out about special postnatal exercise classes.

If you cannot join a class near to home, here are some exercises you could try. Warm up gently before you start and relax afterwards. Repeat each exercise six times to start with, working up to 10 or 12 repetitions. Ask your GP or a physiotherapist for advice if you have any doubts – for example, if an exercise feels too strenuous or you have a previous back or neck injury.

Don't push yourself; short, regular sessions are better than a marathon that tires you out. However keen you are to get your figure back, respect your body and put your baby's needs first.

***Abdominal, Back and
Buttock Exercise***
*1. Kneel on all fours with
your hands pointing for-
wards and your knees hip
width apart.*

*2. Drop your head forwards
and try to touch your face
with one knee. Hold in your
abdominal muscles and
round your back.*

*3. Stretch your leg out
behind you and hold it for a
few seconds, feeling your
buttock muscles tighten.
Repeat the exercise using
your other leg.*

Exercise for Diagonal
Abdominal Muscles
1. Lie with your knees raised
and hands by your sides.

2. Curl your shoulders, touch
opposite fingers, hold and lie
back. Repeat on the other side.

Your postnatal checkup

About six weeks after the birth you'll be offered a check-up, usually with your GP. Your blood pressure and urine will be checked, and your breasts and tummy may be examined. You may be weighed, although many women will not have returned to their pre-pregnancy weight. You'll have an internal examination to make sure that everything is normal, including stitches and the muscle tone in your pelvic floor. A cervical smear may be taken and you'll be asked about your health in general.

Many women have minor discomforts after childbirth. You should discuss anything that is worrying you but on the opposite page there is a list of some common postnatal concerns that you might wish to talk over with your doctor.

Exercise for Straight Abdominal Muscles
1. Sit with your knees raised and a little apart, and your arms stretched out.

2. With your back rounded, curl down a little, hold for a few seconds and curl up again. Keep your muscles controlled.

- Any queries you have about what happened at the birth.
- How you really feel. Your GP cannot be of any help if you smile brightly and say you're feeling fine when you actually feel ill or depressed.
- Uncomfortable tear or episiotomy, sore nipples or any other pain.
- Stress incontinence. Your GP may suggest more pelvic floor exercises (up to 100 a day). If there's little improvement in another six weeks further treatment, such as small weighted cones that you hold in your vagina, may be offered.
- Any difficulties that you're experiencing with your sex life.
- Contraception. You may need a different size of cap or uterine device, or a different pill if you are breastfeeding.

POSTNATAL DEPRESSION

Around 80 per cent of women experience 'baby blues' or some degree of temporary weepiness a few days after the birth. Some women go through a phase of feeling 'down' a few weeks later, when the novelty and excitement surrounding the birth have worn off, sleep deprivation has built up, and there is less practical help from family and friends.

About one woman in 10 suffers moderate postnatal depression, sometimes several months later. Severe depression requiring hospitalization or a long course of treatment affects fewer than one in 500.

Postnatal depression interferes with your enjoyment of life and should always be taken seriously. It's an illness, not a sign of inadequacy, and it's easier to treat if it's caught early. Don't struggle on, failing to recognize the symptoms or feeling too ashamed or lethargic to seek help.

It can be hard to admit to yourself that you feel depressed, especially if you have nothing to be depressed about. There's tremendous pressure to keep up the appearance of coping when everyone else seems to be doing so. If you don't fit the fantasy and nature has not come to your aid and turned you into a competent, contented mother you may feel many negative emotions. These are not signs of an unfeeling monster but of a mother who needs help.

Treatment might consist of individual or group psychotherapy, sessions with a counsellor to talk over your feelings, or a course of anti-depressants. These are not addictive but they usually have to be taken for some time to be effective. When suggesting treatment your GP will take into account your symptoms, your preferences and whether you are breastfeeding. The Association for Postnatal Illness and Meet-A-Mum Association (see Appendix) can also offer support.

POSTNATAL DEPRESSION SYMPTOMS

You may feel low for a few days without being clinically depressed, but it's worth seeking help if you're worried or if you experience any of these symptoms for two weeks:

◆ *An increasing loss of confidence so that you can't face meeting people, even friends, or you need to stick to a rigid routine because you cannot cope with the slightest change.*

◆ *Negative thoughts, feelings of worthlessness or hopelessness.*

◆ *A loss of interest in food, your baby and life in general.*

◆ *Butterflies in your tummy all the time, or a general feeling of panic every time your baby wakes up.*

◆ *An agitated feeling so that you have to keep busy all the time.*

◆ *A feeling of exhaustion but you're unable to sleep when you get the chance.*

Friendship is very important. You and your baby will enjoy sharing the company of other mothers and babies.

MEETING OTHER MOTHERS

The companionship and support of other mothers makes all the difference when you have children. Friends will discuss your baby's development over and over again. They'll understand the joys and difficulties of family life. They'll laugh with you, offer suggestions, reassure you that a phase will pass and find your toddler lovable at times when you secretly find him impossible.

In these early stages it is important to meet and make some new friends. Invite some women from your antenatal class round for coffee – someone has to start the ball rolling. Try looking on your clinic notice board for details of a local parent and toddler group (babies are included). Think about joining a class at your local college, sports or leisure centre – there may well even be a crèche for your baby. Spend time watching the toddlers playing at the local park and chat to the other parents. Ask your health visitor to introduce you to some other mothers. Contact Meet-A-Mum Association or the NCT (see Appendix). They run postnatal groups nationwide.

It's very easy to stay at home and tell yourself that you don't need anything else in your life; to use the possibility that your baby might catch a cold as an excuse for not meeting people. But sooner or later you'll feel lonely, and wish that you and your baby had some friends.

'*I thought I'd work freelance from home, but I hadn't realized just how much time a baby takes up. I hated the thought of someone else looking after Ben and found my career was less important to me than I'd thought! Now I live at a child's pace, not by the clock. I make decisions according to events at the time and ignore the five-year plan that used to rule my life. We can't afford holidays, but now our quality of life is good.*' KATE

RETURNING TO WORK

Returning to work has both positive and negative aspects; just accept this without feeling guilt or any regrets! The popular image of an organized woman with her family life under control so that it never interferes with her work is a myth. The best you can hope for is that your arrangements hold up most of the time. You'll juggle work and motherhood and may feel that you are doing neither job well, but your baby will probably be perfectly happy!

Even if your employer has never considered it before it's worth trying to negotiate a work schedule that suits you. Decide what you want, work out how it could benefit your company, and present your plan to the personnel manager. New Ways to Work (see Appendix) give advice about flexible working practices. You have nothing to lose by taking the initiative.

Parents at Work (see Appendix) have publications on balancing work and home commitments, and choosing childcare. Local social services (see telephone book) keep lists of nurseries and registered childminders. Make arrangements for your return to work in plenty of time and plan a phased handover as peace of mind is very important. Many women carry on breast-feeding night and morning, but allow a week to drop each feed before you start work so that your body can adjust. If your baby won't take a bottle, talk to his carer. He may accept one from her, or he may start to use a beaker.

QUESTIONS AND ANSWERS

Q: I worry about my baby all the time. I even wake him up to make sure he's breathing. I fret over every decision in case it turns out to be wrong. Why am I so twitchy?

A: You worry because you care so much and because your baby still feels part of you. Call it love – or just motherhood!

These feelings can be overwhelming, especially the first time round when each stage your baby goes through is new. You'll gradually learn to relax about day-to-day events as they become familiar, but you may go through phases of intense, stomach-churning anxiety as each new stage arrives.

Babies respond individually so it's rarely possible to be sure that you've made the right decision except with hindsight. This applies whether it's your first baby or your fourth. Experienced mums watch what happens and have no hesitation in changing their mind if a decision proves wrong. If you do your best you'll get it right most of the time.

Q: My hair has been coming out in handfuls since my baby was born. When I brush it more falls out and my pillow is covered with it every morning. What can I do?

A: Hair has growing and resting phases. Pregnancy hormones encourage growth, but when they stop circulating some women's hair stays in the resting phase until the normal growth pattern reasserts itself. Hair loss may start around three to four months after the birth but it usually stops by about six months when the hormone levels stabilize.

Make sure that you get plenty of rest and your diet includes leafy green vegetables. Some people recommend eating seaweeds (from health food shops) to aid normal hair growth.

A small number of women have a continuing problem, so if the loss continues after six months see your GP, who might suggest a private prescription for Regaine, a lotion that is applied to the hair to help regrowth.

Q: My nine-week-old baby has colic. The doctor says she's fine and not to worry, but I'm exhausted breastfeeding her as she's so demanding. Would she settle better on the bottle?

A: A change to bottlefeeding rarely solves the problem, although it may seem to work for a few days. Breast milk consists of foremilk (more dilute and sweet), and hindmilk (richer in fat and more sustaining). Try to space breast-feeds at least two or three hours apart, so that your baby has room in her tummy for both. Between feeds comfort her by cuddling or rocking her. Give her a dummy or your little finger to suck (up to the second joint, fleshy side up). Frequent snacks of foremilk may produce gas so she cries and you give her more foremilk, a vicious circle!

A preparation such as Infacol from the chemist may help, but for most parents the answer is patience. She's not crying because you're doing something wrong; accept this and walk her about. Most babies are more settled when they're three to four months old.

Q: As a single parent, I'm not coping very well with motherhood. I love my daughter but I have no energy and I miss my workmates. How can I start enjoying my life again?

A: Most mothers feel that they are not coping from time to time! Ask your health visitor if she knows a group or another mother whom you could meet. If you do not have any transport other mums may be willing to help out.

Contact Gingerbread and the National Council for One Parent Families (see Appendix) or ask your library for the address of a pen friend group. Borrow a book of action rhymes to enjoy with your daughter, or a pattern book to make something for her.

Even if you don't feel like it at first, making the effort to think beyond chores and to get out and meet people will raise your morale and give you the energy to enjoy life again. Babies are hard work but they are also enormous fun to be with.

APPENDIX

These organizations offer support and information when you are pregnant or have a baby. The Directory of British Organizations (ask at your local library) lists many more groups by subject. Voluntary organizations want their services to be used so don't hesitate to contact them. Many operate nationwide and can put you in touch with your nearest branch, but some are small initiatives run by individuals who give what help they can. Often their services have to be fitted in around family demands, so please offer to phone back at a convenient time and enclose a stamped addressed envelope if requesting information.

UMBRELLA ORGANIZATIONS

Good sources of general information and services, or can put you in touch with the right organization for your needs.

Association for Improvements in the Maternity Services (AIMS), 40 Kingswood Avenue, London NW6 6LS (0181-960 5585). Support and information about maternity rights and options; list of home birth support groups and independent midwives; local groups.

Maternity Alliance, 15 Britannia Street, London WC1X 9JN (0171-837 1265). Over 70 organizations that campaign for parents and babies. Information on health issues, disability and rights at work; booklet about birthplans: 'Your Baby, Your Choice'.

National Childbirth Trust, Alexandra House, Oldham Terrace, London W3 6NH (0181-992 8637). Antenatal classes, postnatal support, breastfeeding counselling, information, study days, leaflets and merchandise. Branches nationwide. ParentAbility offers information and contacts for parents with disabilities.

Regional Health Information Services: Freephone 0800 665544. Can put you in touch with your local health information service for information on health matters; help to find or change any health professional, make a complaint or contact a self-help group; details of the Maternity Services Patient's Charter.

CONCEPTION

Family Planning Association, 27-35 Mortimer Street, London W1N 7RJ (0171-636 7866). Information on fertility, contraception, sexual health, licensed sperm clinics, techniques of sperm separation and achieving a successful pregnancy; addresses of family planning clinics nationwide.

Miscarriage Association, c/o Clayton Hospital, Northgate, Wakefield, W Yorks WF1 3JS (0192-420 0799). Information, support and volunteer contact; local groups.

PREGNANCY

Action on Pre-eclampsia (APEC), 61 Greenways, Abbots Langley Herts WD5 0EU (0192-326 0052). Helpline: 0192-326 6778. Information, support and advice about pre-eclampsia.

Alcohol Concern, Waterbridge House, 32-6 Loman Street, London SE1 0EE (0171-928 7377). Advice for women concerned about their drinking during pregnancy.

British School of Osteopathy, 1-4 Suffolk Street, London SW1Y 4HG (0171-930 9254). List of registered osteopaths; expectant mothers clinic for back/postural problems and massage for labour.

National AIDS Helpline: Freephone 0800 567123. A confidential helpline for anyone concerned about HIV or AIDS. Lines available in various languages; Minicom service for people with hearing/ speech difficulties.

QUIT, Victory House, 170 Tottenham Court Road, London W1P 0HA. Quitline (0171-487 3000) offers counselling; free Quitpacks; referral to local stop smoking groups.

Vegan Society, 7 Battle Road, St Leonards on Sea, East Sussex TN37 7AA (0142-442 7393). Advice about vegan diet during pregnancy.

The Vegetarian Society, Parkdale, Dunham Road, Altrincham, Cheshire WA14 4QG (0161-928 0793). Advice about vegetarian diet during pregnancy.

WellBeing, 27 Sussex Place, Regent's Park, London NW1 4SP (0171-723 9296). Information on nutrition in pregnancy, prematurity, early miscarriage and early diagnosis of fetal abnormalities. Eating in Pregnancy Helpline: 0114-242 4084

Women's Health, 52 Featherstone Street, London EC1Y 8RT (0171-251 6580). Information to help you make informed decisions about your health.

FETAL TESTING

Birth Defects Foundation, Chelsea House, Westgate, London W5 1DR (0181-862 0198). Information and support where a defect, with or without a specific name, is diagnosed.

SATFA (Support Around Termination For Abnormality), 29-30 Soho Square, London W1V 6JB (0171-287 3753). Helpline: 0171-439 6124. Helps parents who discover that their unborn baby is abnormal.

SOFT (Support Organization For Trisomy 13-18 & related disorders), Tudor Lodge, Redwood, Ross-on-Wye, Herefordshire HR9 5UD (0198-956-7480). Information about chromosome disorders; links parents to share experiences; booklet about prenatal diagnosis: 'Your Unborn Baby'.

BIRTH

Active Birth Centre, 55 Dartmouth Park Road, London NW5 1SL (0171-267 3006). Advice, literature and teachers (nationwide) to help you have a natural birth.

Caesarean Support Network, c/o Sheila Tunstall, 2 Hurst Park Drive, Huyton, Liverpool L36 1TF (0151-480 1184). Emotional support and practical advice for women who have had or may need a Caesarean section.

AFTER THE BIRTH

Association for Postnatal Illness (API), 25 Jerdan Place, Fulham, London SW6 1BE (0171-386 0868). Nationwide telephone support for mothers throughout illness by volunteers who have themselves suffered from postnatal illness.

Association of Breastfeeding Mothers, 26 Holmshaw Close, London SE26 4TH (0181-778 4769). Recorded list of breastfeeding counsellors throughout the UK.

CRY-SIS, London WC1N 3XX (0171-404 5011). Parents with a sleepless or excessively crying baby can be put in touch with a telephone volunteer who has experienced a similar problem.

La Leche League (Great Britain) BM 3424, London WC1 3XX (0171-242 1278, 24 hours). Breastfeeding information and support through local groups and telephone counselling.

Meet-A-Mum Association (M.A.M.A.), 14 Willis Road, Croydon CRO 2XX (0181-665 0357). Postnatal support groups and mother to mother support if you have postnatal depression.

National Stepfamily Association, 72 Willesden Lane, London NW6 7TA (0171-372 0844) Helpline: 0171-372 0846. Advice on issues affecting step families.

New Ways to Work, 309 Upper Street, London N1 2TY (0171-226 4026). Information and advice about job sharing and flexible working patterns for individuals and employers.

Parents at Work, 77 Holloway Road, London N7 8JZ (0171-700 5771 Tues, Thurs, Fri 9am-1pm, 2-4pm). Practical advice on work-related issues, including childcare; booklets, workshops, local support groups.

NSPCC Helpline: (0800 800 500, 24 hrs). Practical support for parents who feel they may harm their child.

LONE PARENTS

Gingerbread, 49 Wellington Street, London WC2E 7BN (0171-240 0953). Support for lone parents via a network of self-help groups; advice on holidays and legal and welfare rights.

National Council for One Parent Families, 255 Kentish Town Road, London NW5 2LX (0171-267 1361). Information on issues affecting lone parents; advice for single pregnant women; training courses to help lone parents become financially independent.

BEREAVEMENT

Child Death Helpline: (0171-829 8685). Mon, Thurs, 7-10pm. Weds 10am-1pm. For all those affected by the death of a child from any cause.

Foundation for the Study of Infant Deaths (FSID), 35 Belgrave Square, London SW1X 8QB (0171-235 0965). Helpline (0171-235 1721 (24 hours). Information, advice, support and individual befriending for parents coping with a sudden infant death.

Stillbirth and Neonatal Death Society (SANDS), 28 Portland Place, London W1N 4DE (0171-436 5881). Self help groups and befriending after pregnancy loss, stillbirth or neonatal death; booklet: 'Saying Goodbye to Your Baby'.

SPECIAL SITUATIONS

BLISSLINK-Nippers, 17-21 Emerald Street, London WC1N 3QL (0171-831 9393). Support for parents of babies who are premature or need special or intensive care.

Contact a Family, 170 Tottenham Court Road, London SW1P 0HA (0171-383 3555). Directory of rare conditions and their support networks. Factsheets, parents' guides and telephone helpline.

Council for Disabled Children, 8 Wakley Street, London EC1V 7QE (0171-843 6000) Central co-ordinators of information on all types of help available for disabled children.

Twins and Multiple Births Association (TAMBA), PO Box 30, Little Sutton, South Wirral L66 1TH (0151-348 0020). Twinline: 0173-286 8000, weekdays 6-11pm; weekends 10am-11pm. Local clubs and specialist support for families with twins, triplets or more.

INDEX

ACKNOWLEDGEMENTS

PICTURE CREDITS

COVER PHOTOGRAPH:

SANDRA LOUSADA

ANGELA HAMPTON - FAMILY LIFE PICTURES; 60 top, 136 centre, 137 top, 167 bottom, 167 top, 199

BUBBLES; 94, 134 top and bottom, 135 top and bottom, F. Rombout 2, 34, 64, 82, Ian West 158

CLEFT LIP AND PALATE ASSOCIATION; 170

COLLECTIONS; Anthea Sieveking 92, Sandra Lousada 154

SALLY AND RICHARD GREENHILL; 89, Sally Greenhill 88

ROBERT HARDING PICTURE LIBRARY; S. Villeger 186

HEA BUSINESS UNIT PICTURE LIBRARY; 12

IMAGE BANK; Anthony A. Boccaccio 84

SANDRA LOUSADA; 6

LUPE CUNHA PHOTOGRAPHY; 144, 180

NATIONAL MEDICAL SLIDE BANK; 24, 60 centre

PETIT FORMAT; Taeke Henstra 172

RASCALS; Joanna Mungo 178

REFLECTIONS PHOTO LIBRARY; Jennie Woodcock 48, 126, 139 bottom, 139 top, 176, 182 bottom left, Martin Dohrn 163

SCIENCE PHOTO LIBRARY; David Scharf 22 centre, Petit Format/Nestle 20 , 36 top left, 66 top left, Professors P. M. Motta & J. Van Blerkom 23 top right

TONY STONE IMAGES; Andre Perlstein 8

ZEFA PICTURES LTD; 108

The publishers would like to thank the parents and babies who kindly modelled for this book.